Engagement and Metaphysical Dissatisfaction

Engagement

and

Metaphysical Dissatisfaction

Modality and Value

BARRY STROUD

UNIVERSITY PRESS

2011

OXFORD
UNIVERSITY PRESS

Oxford University Press, Inc., publishes works that further
Oxford University's objective of excellence
in research, scholarship, and education.

Oxford   New York
Auckland   Cape Town   Dar es Salaam   Hong Kong   Karachi
Kuala Lumpur   Madrid   Melbourne   Mexico City   Nairobi
New Delhi   Shanghai   Taipei   Toronto
With offices in
Argentina   Austria   Brazil   Chile   Czech Republic   France   Greece
Guatemala   Hungary   Italy   Japan   Poland   Portugal   Singapore
South Korea   Switzerland   Thailand   Turkey   Ukraine   Vietnam

Published by Oxford University Press, Inc.
198 Madison Avenue, New York, New York 10016

www.oup.com

Oxford is a registered trademark of Oxford University Press

Library of Congress Cataloging-in-Publication Data
Stroud, Barry.
Engagement and metaphysical dissatisfaction : modality and value / by Barry Stroud.
p. cm.
ISBN 978-0-19-976496-9
1. Metaphysics. 2. Causation. 3. Necessity (Philosophy) 4. Value.
I. Title.
BD111.S782   2011
110—dc22   2010013442

1 3 5 7 9 8 6 4 2

Printed in the United States of America
on acid-free paper

For Francesca

If there were a verb meaning 'to believe falsely,' it would not have a meaningful first person present indicative.

—L. Wittgenstein

Contents

Preface

This book deals with three very general and perhaps fundamental ways of thinking about the world, and with what happens when we try to understand those ways of thinking in a certain distinctively philosophical way. Each of those ways of thinking, and the difficulty we face in trying to understand it in that special way, is accorded more or less equal treatment. To maintain that balance across such a wide front I proceed at a very high level of generality. Each way of thinking deserves a more-than-book-length treatment of its own, and over the decades each has been dealt with in that way by many philosophers from different points of view. I do not offer a similarly thorough study here of any of the ways of thinking I consider.

I am interested in thoughts of causal dependence, of necessity, and of the reasons for doing one thing rather than another, and I am equally interested in a certain kind of metaphysical concern with the status of those modal and evaluative thoughts. In identifying and describing the distinctive features of each of those ways of thinking I focus only on some of the simplest, most basic ways they differ from one another and from thoughts of other kinds. Many complexities and implications are therefore left unexplored, even unmentioned. I do not think that threatens the adequacy of the distinctive features I rely on or of the conclusions I draw from them. I describe and defend a very general line of argument that I think links the three ways of thinking and leads to the same conclusion in each case about the prospects of a satisfying metaphysical understanding of them.

One reason these ways of thinking raise special difficulties for metaphysical understanding is that they all appear to be fundamental to human thought as we know it—perhaps essential to any thought of a world and of ourselves as part of a world at all. That possibility, and its implications for a satisfactory metaphysical understanding of the world, are at the very center of my concern. This connects my investigation with Kant's question about the very possibility of metaphysics. But I am interested not only in the special status of whatever conclusions can be reached in metaphysics, but in what kind of understanding we as thinkers can expect to get from metaphysical reflection. Can we achieve the kind of illumination or satisfaction it appears to promise us? On this question I am not as optimistic as Kant.

In these reflections I concentrate on the obstacles I think stand in the way of our reaching the detached, disengaged position we appear to require for a satisfactory metaphysical understanding of ourselves and our thought in relation to an independent world. I try to bring out how and why we cannot expect to achieve such a satisfactory understanding. In earlier epistemological reflections on human knowledge in general, especially in *The Significance of Philosophical Scepticism*, I tried to keep alive the possibility of reaching some such position and seeing from there that no one can ever know anything at all about the world around us. In metaphysical reflection, on the contrary, first in *The Quest for Reality* and now again in this book, I press in the opposite direction, against that possibility. I am not embarrassed by this apparent, and probably real, ambivalence. For one thing, I think the epistemological case is different, and more complex. But ambivalence, or approaching a target at different times from different, even opposed, directions, is perhaps only to be expected in philosophical explorations that search for the real sources of the things that puzzle us rather than seeking to establish philosophical theses or looking for grounds for allegiance to this or that philosophical doctrine. The very idea of a philosophical thesis or doctrine is part of what I wish to investigate.

Like everyone interested in philosophy, I have been encouraged to consider these difficult questions, and helped beyond measure in thinking about them, by a community of philosophers stretching back hundreds of years. Some of the writings I have relied on and responded to here are indicated in the text; others not mentioned are present between the lines. I have tried out parts of this material at different stages of its development in talks and discussions at various places over the last six or seven years and have always gained from the experience. Earlier versions of what is here have been gone over and either taken apart or eventually improved in seminars with acute and persistent Berkeley graduate students. I am grateful to all of them for their interest and their forbearance. It is not possible to mention by name every person who has helped me in one way or another since I first began to think along these lines. I am fully aware that I could not have done what I have done without them. Among those to whom I know I am most recently indebted for specific comments, criticisms, or suggestions I must mention Jason Bridges, John Campbell, Eugene Chislenko, Donald Davidson, Ronald Dworkin, Dina Emundts, Robert Fogelin, Michael Friedman, Hannah Ginsborg, Kerstin Haase, Rolf Peter Horstmann, Niko Kolodny, Gabriele Mras, Thomas Nagel, Christopher Peacocke, Tim Scanlon, Sam Scheffler, Klaus Strelau, Sarah Stroud, and Bernard Williams. I thank them all.

Engagement and Metaphysical Dissatisfaction

1

The Metaphysical Project

However much we come to know or think we know about the world it is possible and sometimes desirable to try to stand back from it and take a more reflective attitude toward our conception of the way things are. We can perhaps even feel a certain general uneasiness in our unexamined acquiescence in familiar and well-entrenched ways of thinking. That we think the world is a certain way is one thing; the world's really being the way we think it is is something different, and something more. This thought alone can be enough to encourage critical assessment of the credentials of our ways of thinking of the world, however familiar and fundamental they might be.

Asking whether things really stand in the world in the ways we think we have good reason to believe they do can be an expression of a human desire to gain a certain kind of satisfying general understanding of ourselves in relation to the world around us. It is in that respect a metaphysical question. Kant thought an urge toward metaphysical understanding is "a natural disposition of human reason," an "inward need" that everyone, or at least every reflective person, feels. He thought we are no more likely to abandon metaphysics in some form or other than we are to decide to stop breathing.[1] The need is not simply general curiosity or a desire to understand ourselves. The metaphysical aspiration Kant had in mind is a desire to understand ourselves in a certain distinctive way.

---

1. Kant, *Prolegomena to Any Future Metaphysics* (ed. G. Hatfield), Cambridge University Press, Cambridge, 2009, p. 118.

The reflections this leads to can proceed in very general terms, about some of the things we all believe or take for granted in everyday life. For instance, we often believe that one thing depends on or happens because of another, or that if a certain thing were to happen a certain other thing would happen as well. A billiard ball goes into a pocket because another ball hits it, or a ball would go into a pocket if it were hit in a certain way. We also accept some things as being necessarily true, with no possibility of their having been otherwise; seven plus five could not possibly have been anything other than twelve. And in doing something we favor one course of action over others, or regard some things as better or more desirable than the alternatives. We eat rather than going to bed, or decide to help someone in distress.

It is possible to find by philosophical reflection that in these thoughts or beliefs or responses we go beyond anything that is strictly speaking so in reality. To put it in more dramatic form, it can be brought home to us that in the world as it is independently of all human beings and their responses to the world, there *are* no dependences between things, no necessary way things absolutely must be, and nothing that is good or bad, better or more desirable than anything else.

This is to be understood in each case as a metaphysical discovery; a conclusion about the way things are. The idea is not just that we can never *know* or be certain or even have good reason to hold any of these everyday beliefs. The causal connections, the necessities, and the value or worth of things that we appear to believe in are said not to be part of independent reality at all. The idea is that it is only something about us and our responses to the world that leads us to think in these distinctive ways, not anything that is so in the world itself that we think about. Metaphysical reflection is meant to reveal how those thoughts and beliefs of ours are really related to the independent world they appear to be about. So it can seem equally possible to be led by metaphysical reflection to reject such negative conclusions and to arrive instead at the positive verdict that the world as it is independently of us and our responses really does contain the kinds of causal connections, or necessities, or worth and value that we ordinarily believe in.

In this book I want to investigate this kind of metaphysical reflec-tion to see how its conclusions are to be reached and what support can be found for them. That is obviously not a task I or anyone could hope to complete. But I want to focus as much as possible on the activity or enterprise of reflecting on ourselves in this way, not simply on what appear to be its results. One element I concentrate on is the beliefs and attitudes we actually have about causation, necessity, and values that the metaphysical conclusions appear to rely on. Can they be understood in a way that supports a satisfying metaphysical con-clusion about them?

My main question is whether or how any active, engaged human per-son who operates with beliefs of those kinds can carry out a reflective philosophical project like this and arrive at metaphysical conclusions he or she can believe and find illuminating. Could anyone who thinks and acts in the world as we all do consistently understand his own and other people's beliefs about causation, necessity, and values as nothing more than what a negative metaphysical verdict about them says they are? And if not, would that give us something we could recognize as positive metaphysical reassurance about the status of those beliefs? Would that put us in a position to declare causal dependence, necessity, and the values of things to be really part of the independent world after all?

I take up these questions in the hope of gaining a better understanding of what metaphysics is or can be and of what we can reasonably expect from it.

One familiar kind of curiosity about our conception of the world can arise out of uncertainty about the support we have for our current beliefs and attitudes. Do we really have good reason to continue to believe all the different kinds of things we believe about the world? Questions of this kind have certainly played a prominent role in philosophical reflec-tion over the years. They are questions about the basis or grounds of our believing or knowing what we do about the world, not simply about our conception of the world itself. Such epistemological questions cannot be kept completely and forever separate from a more directly metaphysical concern with what the world is like, but it is possible, at least for a time, to separate the two. Metaphysical curiosity can express itself even about a conception of the world that we think is as firmly based and well supported as any conception of the world could be.

It is possible to take a certain kind of critical attitude even toward what we take to be knowledge and thoughts and beliefs and feelings acquired from the best sources in the most reliable ways. Metaphysical reflection seeks to subject that whole rich conception of the world to a certain kind of independent scrutiny and assessment. It is to that extent a meta-reflection. It comes after, and reflects critically upon, whatever we have already come to accept in our efforts to make sense of the world. It is an attempt to stand back and not take for granted those parts of our conception of the world that are for the moment under metaphysical scrutiny. Our questions are then directed toward our very conception of the way things are, not to our grounds for holding it.

But the metaphysical aspiration is not simply a desire to know what our conception of the world actually is. Not that an accurate description of our thoughts and attitudes about the world is easily come by, or would be of little interest if we had one. But however thorough and accurate a description of our thoughts and beliefs we came up with, it would not give us the kind of metaphysical understanding I think we seek. It would tell us at best only something about ourselves and our conception of the way things are. But we also want to understand how we and our thoughts about the world stand in relation to a world that is not ourselves. The question is about the relation between the conception we have of the world and the world itself. We hope to ask how things really are in the world by examining the adequacy, accuracy, or comprehensiveness of the conception of the world that we know we have.

It is easy to miss or to misconstrue the distinctively philosophical or metaphysical character of this kind of enterprise. It can look like just one aspect of the attempt to know or understand how things are in general. The logical positivists of the Vienna Circle in the 1930s were not misled by appearances in that way. They drew attention to the very special character of metaphysics and argued against its very possibility on the grounds that it is an expression of a distinctive but unsatisfiable aspiration. For them metaphysics was a search for a kind of knowledge different from anything everyday experience or experimental science could ever provide. It was an attempt to reach above or beyond or somehow behind the best that empirical study of the world can give us, and yet to say something significant about what is really so in the world. For the positivists, the very conception of that task was enough to imply that it could not possibly succeed.

One thing I think the logical positivists were right about was their recognition that metaphysics is not just one among many different ways of studying the world. It is a special and distinctively *philosophical* study of the way things are. And on the positivists' map of all possible varieties of human knowledge there was simply no place for any such philosophical study. That map made room only for empirically verifiable propositions about the world on the one hand and propositions that can be seen to be necessarily and so 'analytically' true on the other. Philosophy was not an empirical study of the world, so any knowledge it might come up with could find its place on that map only as the 'analysis' of something else that could also find a place there. Philosophy could yield at best only 'analytic' knowledge that is therefore 'empty of factual content,' and so completely silent about how things actually are. But the neat dividing lines of that suspiciously simple map of human knowledge have themselves been brought into question, not least by the undying force of the metaphysical aspiration itself.

The anti-metaphysical positivists wanted to eliminate what they regarded as mere 'pseudo-questions' or empirically unsettleable and so unreal 'disputes' that only seem to be about the way things are. Such apparent questions are empirically completely idle, with no possible criteria for settling them one way or the other, so no putative 'answers' to them could be part of what anyone could know. Speculation and elaborate intellectual construction beyond the limits of all possible verification might offer pleasant or even reassuring pictures of the world and our position in it, but it could give us nothing that anyone could have reason to believe.

Like the logical positivists who came after him, Kant had not thought highly of what metaphysics had been able to achieve in the past either. And he saw no hope for the future in anything like the kind of speculative reflection metaphysics had engaged in up till his time. But Kant thought "to forego [metaphysics] entirely is impossible," so he tried to work out the only way in which the kind of satisfaction we seek can be achieved. He sought to lay down once and for all the conditions of the possibility of any metaphysical knowledge or understanding of the world. The key was to investigate the conditions of our having the very thoughts and knowledge of the world that we want to subject to metaphysical assessment.

What Kant prescribed along these lines is an enterprise of forbidding complexity. But it has one feature that it seems to me any metaphysical inquiry worth taking seriously must have. It is what might be called metaphysics *from within*. It starts with the thoughts and beliefs we actually have about the world and investigates the conditions of our having them. Even if it turns out that no illuminating metaphysical conclusions can finally be reached, there seems to be no alternative to at least beginning in this way. Unless we are prepared to make everything up as we go along, we have no choice but to start from where we are now, with what we already believe and think we know about the world, and see if metaphysical reflection on that conception can yield reliable new understanding of what is really so.

This kind of reflection promises a conception of reality that is an improvement of what we start with. We start out from everything we believe or have any opinions about and ask how much of that body of belief, or what parts of it, express something that is actually so in the world we take those beliefs and attitudes to be about. Whatever is found to pass the test receives positive metaphysical assessment; it will have been found (by our best philosophical lights) to be part of what is really so in the world. Ways we think things are that are found to fail the test in one way or another will have been exposed as not really capturing anything that is so in the world after all, or at least not capturing what they might have seemed to capture before metaphysical reflection. The goal is to achieve an enhanced—a metaphysically corrected—conception of what the world is like. It is meant to tell us, contrary to the way we (perhaps uncritically) took things to be at the beginning, how things really are.

What looks like a simple and uncontroversial example of this kind of thinking is expressed in the familiar adage "Beauty lies only in the eye of the beholder." Most of us think that there are many beautiful things in the world, or at least that some things are more beautiful than others. We seek that beauty, and enjoy it when we find it. Of course beauty can take many different forms. But when we ascribe beauty to things of different kinds we appear to believe that, for all their differences, the things are nonetheless beautiful, each in its own way. The familiar maxim says that what we appear to think and say in making such judgments cannot be taken for granted as giving the best understanding of what is really so when we think and speak about beauty in those ways. The maxim purports to cut below the surface of our accepted ways of thinking and speaking about the beauty of things to give an improved or corrected understanding of the relation between those thoughts or beliefs we express and the world they are in some sense about.

The observation that beauty lies only in the eye of the beholder can be seen as metaphysical in purporting to tell us what the world to which we appear to ascribe beauty is really like or what it really contains. Or rather it tells us what the world does *not* really contain. It says the world does not really contain any objects that have a property of being beautiful or more beautiful than other objects. More precisely, it says that no objects have any such property independently of all "beholders'" responses to them. Beauty is *only* in the eye of the beholder; it is not something possessed by any objects independently of the responses that lead beholders to call them beautiful.

This conclusion is and is meant to be negative or deflating in a certain respect. It says that beauty is *only* something or other, not everything we might perhaps have thought it is. It gives beauty a certain dependent status by placing it on one side of what can be seen as a dividing line between "beholders" and their responses to the world on the one hand and the world on the other side of that line that is as it is independently of anyone's responses to it. However things might otherwise be on their own on the far side of that line—independently of all conscious subjects and their responses—there are no beautiful objects, according to this picture. Nor, for the same reason, are there any ugly objects either. Something that we "beholders" appear to think or imply in saying that a thing is beautiful or ugly is denied or taken away or somehow qualified by this metaphysical verdict. It says that whether something is beautiful or not, and what sort of thing the beauty we all appear to believe in is, depends on something that is true only of "us"—something on the "beholders'" side of the dividing line.

It is easier to feel that you get the general point behind this familiar maxim than it is to formulate a reasonably clear and defensible version of it that reveals exactly how our thoughts of and responses to the beauty of things go beyond or in some other way fail to capture what is so in the independent world. That is partly because we do not at the moment possess an accurate account of how we actually think of and respond to the beauty of things, and it would not be easy to come up with such a description. But even if we had one it would not be enough to reveal the metaphysical point. We would also need a conception of what the world is really like on its own, independent of all human thoughts and responses. Only then could we appreciate the relation between the way we think things are in our thoughts about beauty and the way things really are. We could then understand how beauty as we think of it fits into the world described by a metaphysically purified conception that includes only what is really so.

Getting into position to make such a discovery is a more complicated task than it might look. We do not begin metaphysical reflection about beauty with an already-formulated conception of how things really are. If we did, we could simply consult that conception of the world to see how our thoughts and responses about beauty fit into it. But we cannot start there. We can achieve such a purified conception of independent reality, if at all, only by starting with everything we think and feel about the whole world, including our beliefs about the beauty of things, and somehow precipitating out of that totality something we can regard as a metaphysically corrected or improved conception of what is really so. That step is unavoidable, given what I have called metaphysics from within; we must start with everything we accept and refine it down to what we can see to be really so. So even to arrive at a conception of independent reality against which to assess the status of beauty as we think of it we would need an accurate understanding not only of our thoughts about beauty, but of all our other ways of thinking of and responding to the world as well.

It is perhaps easy to feel that we do not really need to engage in such elaborate reflections in order to grasp the basic point of the familiar maxim about beauty. I think there is a strong presumption that, whatever our ways of thinking about beauty turned out to be, and whatever the world fully independent of us happened to be like, beauty could not really be anything other than *some* kind of byproduct of "beholders'" responses to a beauty-free independent world. It is easy to feel not only that the traditional maxim is basically right, but that beauty could not really be anything else; that it must lie somehow only in the "eye" of the beholder.

I think it is worth trying to get to the bottom of this kind of feeling or reaction. I would like to understand where such a strong sense of meta-physical conviction comes from and what lies behind it. What makes it seem simply undeniable about beauty, or about anything else? How does this special kind of metaphysical insight or reflection work, and what can reasonably be expected from it?

In later chapters I try to determine, with respect to three of our most fundamental and pervasive ways of thinking of the world, whether it is possible to find either that those thoughts or attitudes go beyond every-thing that is strictly speaking so in reality or, on the contrary, that the world really is as we take it to be in those respects. Can we carry out this kind of reflective project and consistently reach a metaphysically satis-fying conclusion? Can we find that there is nothing in independent reality corresponding to fundamental beliefs and attitudes we know we have? And if we cannot, does that give us positive metaphysical reassur-ance that the world really is as those beliefs and attitudes represent it to be after all?

The apparently uncontroversial case of beauty seems to support at least the general feasibility of some such project. But to reach any satis-factory metaphysical outcome even in that case we would need good answers to three interconnected questions. The first question is how it is known or how it is to be established that the metaphysical verdict is correct. What shows that beauty is only in the eye of the beholder and is nothing present on its own in the world as it is fully independently of all beholders' responses? This question is often simply ignored. It can seem obvious or beyond question that beauty itself could be nothing in the independent world. But finding or declaring it obvious is just another expression of the metaphysical conviction that the traditional maxim about beauty simply must be right. It is not an independent reason in support of that conclusion.

Widespread and apparently irresolvable disagreements about the beauty of things are often invoked in support of the maxim. But dis-agreements, even wide cultural differences, alone are not enough. It depends as well on what explains whatever differences there are. Further support might come from the idea not just that people disagree but that there is no possible way to settle the questions of beauty on which they differ. That in turn can easily lead to the conclusion that there is no real question at issue in judgments of beauty—that there is nothing in the world for different beholders to be right or wrong about. That is in effect what the traditional maxim about beauty says or implies. But what shows that it is not possible to settle the question of a thing's beauty, or that there is no such thing in the world to be right or wrong about?

It will perhaps be said that it is impossible to settle the question because judgments of beauty are judgments of taste. And, according to another familiar maxim, there is no disputing matters of taste. This cannot mean that people do not in fact dispute matters involving taste, since they do it all the time. It is true that judgments of beauty do require a certain taste or distinctive sensitivity on the part of those who make them. But some distinctive sensitivities or discriminative capacities are required for virtually every judgment we make. We could not even perceive the shapes or sizes of the objects around us if we did not have the appropriate perceptual sensitivities. But that does not suggest that the shapes and sizes of the things we perceive lie only in the eye or other sense organ of the beholder, or that the objects that cause those perceptions do not really have shapes or sizes.

Perhaps the maxim about beauty rests rather on the idea that *nothing more* than the effects objects have on our minds or sensibilities is relevant to the judgments we make about the beauty of things—that the "beholders'" responses themselves are enough to account for all the differences among different judgments of beauty. This rests on a certain understanding of what people say or think when they make judgments of beauty. It says that in declaring something to be beautiful we do no more than express a certain feeling or reaction we have to the thing, or we announce or describe a feeling we have toward it. If judgments of beauty are to be understood in this way, the feelings or responses in question would have to be specified more fully; not just any reaction we have to something is relevant to our regarding it as beautiful. But if the appropriate feelings or responses could be accurately specified, this way of understanding our judgments of beauty would support the conclusion that there is nothing in the independent world for different judgers of beauty to disagree about. Whether something is beautiful or not would depend on how human beings do or would respond to it. It could then be said, with admissible license, that the beauty they speak of lies only in the eyes of beholders.

But is this actually true of our judgments of beauty? This is a question about what we actually say or think or judge in speaking of the beauty of things. This is the second of the three questions to be asked about this kind of metaphysical enterprise. It is the question of what the thoughts or beliefs that are subject to metaphysical assessment are really like, and how they work. We need a correct answer to this question in order to accept the traditional maxim about the beauty we believe in. What *do* we say or think or judge when we declare things to be beautiful?

I said that this is not an easy question to answer. But for all its difficulty, it appears to be a more or less straightforward question of fact. It is a question to which anyone who would reach a reliable metaphysical verdict about beauty must have an answer, since that verdict purports to tell us something about the relation between our ways of thinking and speaking about beauty on the one hand and a reality that is independent of us and our responses on the other. The acceptability of any metaphysical conclusion arrived it in this way therefore depends on whether what it says or implies about our actual ways of thinking can be seen to be correct. Metaphysical reflection directed toward ways of thinking that are not the ways we actually think of the world would yield at best an assessment of some other thoughts and beliefs, not ours. It could not give us the illumination we seek about our own conception of the world. At worst it would not be an assessment of anyone's actual thoughts or beliefs at all, but simply a declaration that the world really is a certain way. That is the kind of thing that gives metaphysics a bad name.

As a matter of fact it seems to me that in declaring something to be beautiful we are not typically simply expressing or even describing a feeling we have in response to the thing. We do often have certain feelings in the presence of a beautiful object, many of which are aroused by the object itself, but in saying or thinking that the object is beautiful we appear to be predicating something of the object or thinking of it in a certain way. What we ascribe to the object in those assertions seems to be just what we ask or wonder about when we ask or wonder whether a certain object is beautiful. We can ask that question about an object that is nowhere near us and from which we get no relevant feelings one way or the other at the moment. We ask or wonder whether the object has what we would ascribe to it if we were to think it is beautiful.

Perhaps in ascribing beauty to something we can be understood to ascribe to it a tendency or power to produce feelings or reactions of certain kinds in us or in certain kinds of perceivers. That is something an object can have whether anyone is actually perceiving it or not. This too, if the appropriate feelings could be accurately specified, would be consistent with the traditional maxim about beauty. Whether an object has such a power or not depends in part on what the perceivers whose feelings or responses are relevant are like. If "beholders" had been different in certain ways from the ways they actually are now, objects that now have the power to affect perceivers in certain ways would not have had the power to do that. So on this understanding of judgments of beauty, whether something is beautiful or not would depend on what certain perceivers are like, and so in that sense the beauty would lie only in the eye of the beholder.

But perhaps our most considered judgments of beauty are to be understood in some other way. Could it be that in ascribing beauty to an object we predicate of it a property or feature that we do not regard as completely explainable or definable solely in terms of the responses of beholders or of an object's power to produce them? This would not mean that the feelings or reactions we have to objects we regard as beautiful are not important, even essential. But on this kind of view those feelings, or the prospect of our getting them, would be something that leads us to think of objects as beautiful and to seek beauty and to enjoy it when we find it, but it would not be what we ascribe to an object in speaking of it as beautiful in the ways we do. In thinking of an object as beautiful we could be thinking of it as having some quality or feature that is not explainable in terms of feelings or responses alone. Its beauty could be something different from its having a tendency to produce certain responses, even though it does have such a tendency. We would then be predicating of objects we regard as beautiful something that is not equivalent or fully reducible to anything that is true only of beholders or of the powers objects have to produce them.

Whether we do think and speak of beautiful things in this way—and if we do, what we thereby say and think about them—is a factual question about our judgments of beauty: what do we actually say or think in ascribing beauty to something? It is the second of what I have called the three critical questions. The effort to answer this question in the right way is what raises the third question. Reaching a negative metaphysical conclusion about beauty requires that we be able to find that the description of our ways of thinking of the beauty of things that the metaphysical reflection relies on is actually correct. We must be able to recognize ourselves and our actual beliefs and responses in the ways of thinking that the project subjects to metaphysical assessment. And we must be able to find that description correct prior to and independently of accepting any particular metaphysical verdict. The acceptability of such a verdict depends in part on the accuracy of the description given of our thought in the reflection that is meant to lead to that verdict.

The third question to be asked is whether we can find that we do in fact think of and respond to beauty in the ways the metaphysical reflection depends on and at the same time accept what the metaphysical verdict says: that there is no such thing as beauty in the world independently of all beholders' responses to things. This is not simply a question of whether two different propositions are consistent or not. It is not the question whether it could be true that we all think there are many beautiful things in the world even though there are in fact no beautiful things in the world. It is perfectly possible for us to believe something even though it is not true. What I want to bring into question is whether we who reflect on our thoughts and beliefs in the ways I have been describing can find it possible to *accept* both that we do think of the world in those ways and that the world is not that way.

Can we find ourselves in a position to accept both what the metaphysical verdict says about our ways of thinking of the beauty of things and what it says about the way things really are? This is a question about the prospects of metaphysical reflection and the consequences of trying to accept its apparent results. It is about the outcome of a metaphysical assessment of the status of something we take ourselves to believe in, or the kind of illumination or satisfaction that can be expected from it. This is the kind of question I want to draw special attention to.

I think it can easily seem that this question presents no special obstacle in the case of beauty in particular. There would seem to be no difficulty for anyone who thinks that in saying that something is beautiful we simply express or describe a certain kind of feeling or response we have or would have to the thing, or that we attribute to the object a power to produce such responses. To accept such an account of our judgments of beauty would make it possible to accept the negative metaphysical verdict about beauty while continuing to engage in the practice of thinking and speaking of the beauty of things in the ways it says we do. We would have come to see that the presence of beauty as we actually think and speak of it does depend in some way or other on something that is true of beholders.

Even finding that our judgments of beauty cannot be fully explained in any of those ways—as nothing more than expressions of beholders' responses or the disposition of some objects to produce them—would not necessarily present an obstacle to accepting the negative metaphysical verdict. We might find by careful reflection that in judgments of beauty we do in fact typically ascribe to the object some characteristic we think of as different from and not explainable in terms of facts about perceivers' feelings and responses alone. We might find that we regard beauty as something different, and something more, than all such facts about "beholders." On this kind of view, the beliefs we accept about the beauty of things would conflict with the metaphysical verdict that says there is no beauty in the world independently of all beholders and their responses. We could not consistently accept the beliefs that this account says we actually hold about the beauty of things and at the same time accept that negative metaphysical verdict about beauty.

This of course is so far only an inconsistency; it does not mean that we could not accept the metaphysical verdict. In fact, accepting a particular metaphysical verdict can even lead us to reject what is in fact a correct understanding of our ways of thinking, or what otherwise would have been the most plausible way of understanding them. We might reject an account of our thought precisely because accepting it is not compatible with accepting what the metaphysical verdict says. This shows why it is important for the answer to our second question—how do we actually think of the beauty of things?—to be arrived at first, independently of our having accepted any metaphysical verdict about the contents of those judgments. Metaphysical conviction can lead in this way to distortion or misunderstanding of what we actually say and believe even in the most familiar everyday judgments we are trying to understand. For metaphysical reflection to illuminate our actual thoughts about the world it must proceed in the opposite direction.

But even if we find that we do in fact think of the beauty of things as something different from everything the negative metaphysical verdict says is part of reality, it would still be possible for us to accept that negative verdict about beauty. What we could not consistently do is accept that verdict while continuing to accept the everyday beliefs we hold about the beauty of things. On the way of understanding those beliefs that we are now considering, the negative metaphysical verdict implies that none of those beliefs, so understood, would be true. What they attribute to objects is something that that metaphysical verdict says is not possessed by any objects in the world.

If we continued to think and speak about the beauty of things as this view says we now do, and if we also accepted the negative metaphysical verdict about beauty, we would have to see ourselves in our judgments of beauty as believing things that the metaphysical theory we accept says are not true. We could not fully, or in full awareness, endorse those judgments. We would be committed to a doctrine that regards them as not true in the way we understand them. Of course, as soon as we moved away from metaphysical reflection and immersed ourselves once again in the world around us, we might easily fall right back into thinking and saying the kinds of things we have always thought about the beauty of things. But in accepting the negative metaphysical verdict we could not seriously defend that practice or the truth of what we say when engaging in it. Our own best reflection on what we do and on what is so in the world would have exposed all those beliefs as error or illusion on a grand scale. To accept that metaphysical conclusion while continuing to make judgments of beauty would not be a satisfactory position to find oneself in. If we simply cannot help making judgments of beauty, it would be to find that we cannot help believing things that we are convinced simply cannot be true.

It would perhaps be possible to free ourselves from this ironic or whimsical condition and continue to use the *words* 'beauty' and 'beautiful' as we have in the past while now thinking of them as really serving only to draw attention to the feelings we do or would get from certain objects, or perhaps to the powers objects have to produce them. We might utter the same words as before while understanding what we thereby say in ways we can see to be consistent with the negative metaphysical verdict about beauty. We continue to speak of the sun as rising in the east and falling below the western horizon while accepting a theory according to which the sun does not move.

Acceptance of the negative metaphysical verdict about beauty could have even more far-reaching effects. It could change not only our understanding of our practice of speaking and thinking of the beauty of things, but that very practice itself. If we remain convinced that the everyday judgments we have been making of the beauty of things do imply and so commit us to something that the negative metaphysical verdict says is not really part of the independent world, we could resolve not to make such over-committal judgments of beauty any longer. We could try to abandon what we would have seen to be a benighted enterprise. Enlightened persons have often been led to abandon practices and ways of thinking that they have come to see as repositories of error and illusion.

But the conflict might equally lead us to look again at what we took to support the metaphysical verdict in the first place, or what makes us so confident of its correctness. There would be good reason to do this if we think the beauty we ascribe to objects as things are now is not in fact something we regard as equivalent or reducible to anything that the more austere metaphysical view would acknowledge as part of independent reality. In the absence of further argument, why should we be more willing, in the face of a negative metaphysical verdict, to abandon the judgments of beauty we already accept than to abandon a metaphysical verdict that conflicts with those judgments? What is the source of the sense that metaphysics has a stronger claim to correctness or illumination than what we accept as part of the world without any metaphysical help?

If we remain convinced of the negative metaphysical verdict about beauty for whatever reason, abandoning all everyday judgments of beauty that conflict with it will perhaps seem like the most satisfactory metaphysical outcome. By no longer speaking of beauty in those old ways or attributing it to objects around us, we would have brought our thought and practice into line with what our best metaphysical reflection reveals is really true of the world we think about. This would seem to represent genuine philosophical progress—just the kind of illumination and self-understanding that metaphysics appears to promise. By reflection on our actual ways of thinking we would have come to understand more clearly how we actually think of the beauty of things and so how to free ourselves from the errors and confusions about beauty that we now find we have been victims of in the past.

This need not alter or obliterate all the elaborate feelings and responses we have always had toward things we regard as beautiful. Those feelings and responses themselves, and the objects that cause them, would remain part of what the austere metaphysical theory regards as reality, so there would be no need to deny them. Rather than (as we would now see it) falsely ascribing something called beauty to the objects we take an interest in, it looks as if we could just talk more directly about the feelings and responses those objects produce in us and leave it at that. If we still retained some distinctive ways of marking and attending to the special interest and attractiveness that certain kinds of objects have always had for us, we might feel that nothing had really been lost. After all, according to the negative metaphysical verdict about beauty, if we thought and spoke in only these new and corrected ways we would not be missing anything that is actually so in reality.

I think it is still an open question whether such satisfying philosophical illumination can ever really be reached even in the case of beauty. Many believe it has already been achieved in that case. I think we could be confident of such a reassuring outcome only if we had a better understanding than I think we do of how our judgments of beauty actually work and what attitudes we actually hold toward objects we regard as beautiful. That is a daunting question to which I think we still do not have a convincing answer. I introduce the case of beauty here not to pursue it further but only to illustrate the general structure of the kind of metaphysical enquiry I am interested in. It can serve to indicate what is required to achieve a finally satisfactory metaphysical outcome even in a case that many have long regarded as completely uncontroversial.

In the rest of this book I take up three areas of our thought about the world that are more central and so more fundamental than our views about the beauty of things. I want to see what support can be found there for metaphysical conclusions that would take away or deny something we appear to believe in. In each case I think we face special obstacles in getting even as far toward satisfying metaphysical conclusions as we can seem to get in the case of beauty. There is an elusive but persistent kind of dissatisfaction it is possible to feel in the face of each of these efforts at metaphysical understanding. I want to identify some of the source of that dissatisfaction and try to understand and explain why what we feel we seek must remain unattainable. This might eventually lead us to wonder whether seeking the kind of metaphysical satisfaction I have been trying to identify is the best way to proceed in philosophy. Maybe not being able to reach that metaphysical goal, while understanding why we cannot have what we feel we want, is the most we can hope for. Maybe it could even offer a different kind of philosophical under-standing of ourselves.

Whatever support can be found for such metaphysical conclusions in these central areas must be found in the only place it makes sense to look for it first—in the beliefs and other attitudes we actually have about causal dependence, necessity, and values. That is a huge subject—three huge subjects, in fact. There is no question of my doing full justice to any one of them, let alone to all three. But I think considering each of these areas side by side with the others promises greater understanding of the general metaphysical enterprise they are all part of, and perhaps a better estimate of its prospects of success in any one of them.

There are two general reasons for doubt about reaching satisfying metaphysical conclusions in these central areas of our thought. First, there is good reason to think that each of the fundamental concepts in question is irreducible to any set of concepts that does not presuppose it. They cannot be fully explained in different but equivalent terms. If that is so, anyone who understands and recognizes that we have the beliefs about causation, necessity, and values that are to be subjected to metaphysical assessment must therefore possess those very concepts himself and have thoughts and beliefs involving them. Accepting a neg-ative metaphysical verdict that denies that the concepts in question apply to anything in the independent world would directly conflict with accepting any beliefs of those kinds.

If our beliefs about the beauty of things were irreducible to other terms in this way, and we were faced with this kind of conflict, it would seem possible as a last resort simply to abandon our beliefs about the beauty of things. But that does not appear to be a possible option here, with our beliefs in causation, necessity, and values. That is because beliefs or attitudes of those three central kinds have a strong claim to be regarded not only as irreducible but also as indispensable for any thought at all, or at least for the kind of thinking involved in a metaphysical assessment of their status. That is something to be explored and defended in each case in the chapters that follow. If it is right, the indispensability of those ways of thinking stands in the way of the detachment or disengagement that appears to be needed for genuine metaphysical illumination. It would represent an obstacle to our getting far enough outside our acceptance of the beliefs and attitudes in question to assess their metaphysical credentials with the appropriate neutrality. This is not only a threat to the possibility of metaphysically unmasking these fundamental beliefs as not capturing anything that is so in the independent world. It also casts doubt on the prospects of any appropriately positive reassurance about their independent metaphysical status.

Trying to accept a negative metaphysical verdict about irreducible ways of thinking that we simply cannot abandon leads to dissatisfaction or instability. If the beliefs are indeed indispensable, we will continue to make judgments of those very kinds. In accepting a negative metaphysical verdict about them we would therefore understand ourselves to believe something that the theory we also accept says is not true or does not capture anything that is so in the world. This is not a stable position. The instability does not imply that the metaphysical theory we accept is not or cannot be true. But accepting such a theory about what we believe while continuing to believe what we cannot avoid believing would leave us in a continuously dissatisfying predicament. We could not achieve the kind of understanding of our irreducible and indispensable ways of thinking that this kind of metaphysical reflection seems to promise.

Ways of thinking that are irreducible and indispensable for thinking of any world at all would be shown in this way to enjoy a certain kind of invulnerability against metaphysical exposure. In what follows I explore different varieties or degrees of this indispensability and try to assess the nature and extent of whatever metaphysical invulnerability it can be seen to provide. The question is whether under any proper understanding of these central and fundamental ways of thinking we could consistently achieve the satisfaction that this kind of metaphysical reflection aspires to.

2

Causation

We make sense of things that happen by coming to believe that one thing was caused to happen by another thing that happened, or that it happened because something else happened. We can believe that a certain thing would not have happened if certain other things had not happened. In deciding what to do on a particular occasion we can reflect that if we were to do so-and-so then such-and-such would happen, and we act accordingly, depending on what we want. We could not deliberate and act for considered reasons as we do if we did not have thoughts and beliefs of these kinds about one thing being connected or dependent on another.

Beliefs of these kinds all involve more than the thought of one thing's happening and another thing's happening. They involve a further idea of some kind of connection or dependence between things. We think of the two things, or of the relation between them, in a different way, or in a different modality, from the mere conjunction of their both happening. Something additional or stronger is expressed in saying 'b happened because a happened' than in the mere conjunction 'a happened and b happened.' Dependence of this kind does not require that anything of either kind actually happen. It is present in the so-called counterfactual or subjunctive conditional 'If something F were to happen something G would happen,'[1] which is not implied by the simple regularity 'Whenever

---

1. Neither of these familiar labels for statements of this kind is strictly correct. The antecedent of the conditional need not be false or 'counter' or contrary to fact, and only the antecedent of the whole conditional statement is typically in the subjunctive, with the consequent in the conditional mood.

there is an F there is a G.' If there is never an F at all it is true that there is never an F without a G, or that whenever there is an F there is a G. But there being no Fs at all does not imply that if there were an F there would be a G.

I will not try to define 'causation' or 'causal connection' or 'dependence.' I will speak also of 'laws of nature' or 'law-like connections' and 'counterfactual' or 'subjunctive' conditionals, but without suggesting that any of those terms is (or is not) fully definable in terms of any of the others. I am interested in a feature I think is common to all of them: the distinctive modality of thoughts expressing a kind of dependence between things or states of affairs.

The further or different modality that figures in those thoughts has been found problematic, even mysterious. Many philosophers have denied that we can make full sense of it. Others grant that we have some such idea but deny that it actually applies to anything in the independent world. The best-known philosopher who appears to have said both these things is Hume, and a great many others down to our own day follow him on one point or the other, and for what look like broadly Humean reasons. The special modality involved in causal or subjunctive conditional thoughts has accordingly been regarded as at best an expression of an attitude we take to the world, or a reflection of our ways of thinking about it, not something that holds in the world we thereby think about.

Hume agrees that we think of causation as involving some kind of necessary connection or dependence between cause and effect. It is not simply the idea of one thing following another, or the idea of all things of one kind always following something of a certain other kind. We think that, for two things related as cause and effect, if the first occurs the second not just will but *must* occur. It is brought about or produced by its cause. But for Hume the ideas of necessity or power or efficacy or dependence that we employ in such thoughts "represent not any thing, that does or can belong to the objects, which are constantly conjoin'd."[2] He insists that "Upon the whole, necessity is something, that exists in the mind, not in objects, nor is it possible for us ever to form the most distant idea of it, consider'd as a quality in bodies."[3] I take this to be a

---

2. D. Hume, *A Treatise of Human Nature* (ed. L. A. Selby-Bigge), Oxford University Press, Oxford, 1978, p. 164.

3. Hume, *Treatise*, pp. 164–165. This remark can be misunderstood. In saying that "necessity is something, that exists in the mind, not in objects" Hume did not mean that there *are* necessary connections between things that happen in the mind

negative metaphysical verdict about causal dependence. The distinctive modality of statements of such dependence is said to express
nothing that is present in the world independently of all human
responses to it.

What reasons there might be for holding this metaphysical view, and
how good those reasons are, is not easy to say. Hume's celebrated treatment concentrates primarily on what he calls the *idea* of causation: what
is that idea, and how do we get it? He starts from the observation that we
never *perceive* any necessity or dependence with which one event follows another in any particular instance; we get no 'impression' of any
such connection. He thinks we do get an *idea* of a causal connection
between things, and so can come to *think* things are connected, after we
have observed many instances of something of one kind always followed
by something of a certain other kind. But the source of that new idea or
thought is to be found in something that happens in our minds during
that series of exactly resembling perceptions, and not in any connection
or dependence we perceive in any particular instance. The origin of the
idea, and hence of the beliefs we express with it, lies in us, not in the
independent world.

Despite the enormous influence Hume's views have had on the understanding of causal necessity or dependence, this way of arriving at a
negative metaphysical verdict of the "fictional" character of our thought
about it does not turn on anything distinctive or uniquely problematic
about causation in particular. It rests in large part on a completely general theory of perception according to which the most anyone can ever
perceive is extremely limited in comparison with what we eventually
come to think about the world on the basis of the "fleeting and momen-
tary" impressions we receive. On that view we perceive only certain
features within the passing show of the personal experience of each of
us. We never, strictly speaking, perceive anything that continues to exist
for any significant length of time. So we perceive no physical objects or
any of the other enduring things we believe the world contains. This
theory of perception therefore makes the independent existence of
everything we believe as problematic as Hume thinks causal dependence is. We never perceive any such things to be so. Almost all our

---

but not between any other kinds of objects. To read him that way would be like taking
the remark 'Beauty lies only in the eye of the beholder' to mean that the only beautiful
things in the world are beholders' eyes. Hume meant rather that there are no necessary
connections between things anywhere; we only *think* there are because of what
happens in our minds when we observe certain things that happen in the world.
The connections are "in our minds" and not in the world in the sense in which all
"fictions" are only "in our minds" and not in the world.

beliefs about anything can therefore be accounted for only by appeal to something that happens in our minds when we receive our rudimentary impressions, not to anything we can ever perceive to be so in the world we come to believe in.

Many philosophers of more recent times remain in a broad sense followers of Hume on the status of causation without accepting such a severely restricted conception of the scope of perception. They appear to hold that we can perceive and thereby have a conception of physical objects and other enduring things and states of affairs even though the idea of causal dependence between such things in the independent world remains problematic or metaphysically dubious. The source of their doubts is not easy to determine. One possible source is the assumption that we never perceive instances of causal connection or dependence. A different but related possibility is that causal dependence is thought to be unperceivable because of the doubtful intelligibility of the idea of such a connection. In any case, it certainly is still widely believed that we never perceive causal connections between things. By now the view is hardly ever argued for. The most that is usually offered in its support is a reverential bow in the direction of Hume, but with no acknowledgment of the restrictive theory of perception that Hume's own denial rests on.

Whatever might seem to count in favor of the idea that we cannot perceive instances of causal dependence, it has very implausible, not to say disastrous, consequences that have not been squarely faced.[4] If we never perceived causal connections between things, or never perceived that things are causally connected, we could never see a stone *break* a window or see one billiard ball *knock* another ball into a pocket. Nor could we ever see that the second ball went into the pocket *because* the first one hit it. We would never see a person *push* a door open, or closed, and never see anyone *pick up* a knife or fork—or *do* anything else, for that matter. The most we could be said to see of a stone's breaking a window on this view would be a stone's reaching a place where there is a window and then seeing many flying pieces of what used to be a window. Even that is probably going too far. Without being able to see one thing's depending on another could we even see a stone *reach* a certain place or see something that *used to be* part of a window?

---

4. Doubts about the unperceivability of causal connections are expressed and forcefully defended by, e.g., G. E. M. Anscombe, "Causality and Determination," in her *Collected Papers*, vol. 2, *Metaphysics and Philosophy of Mind*, University of Minnesota Press, Minneapolis, 1981.

This raises a general question about how or whether a person could think about and understand the objects this view admits that we do see. Could we have a conception of a world of visible, enduring objects at all if we could never see what any of those objects do, or see them doing it? Hume's actual view does not face this difficulty. He thinks not only that we never see a stone break a window, but that we never see a stone or a window either. Hume acknowledges the need to explain how we get even so much as the idea of an enduring object from the fleeting perceptions we receive, and how we come to think of such things as perceivable. But for those who think we can see an object and know what it is and where it is and what will happen if certain other things happen, but that we never *see* the object doing or undergoing any of the things it does, there is a special problem. That view denies that we ever see a billiard ball knock another ball into a pocket or see a person push a door open or pick up a knife and fork. Could we think of and understand objects like billiard balls and persons as we do if we could never perceive them doing the kinds of things we believe they can do?

This begins to bring out the fundamental importance of the idea of causal dependence in our thought about the world. To think of any such world at all requires a capacity to think of an order of things independent of our perceptions of them: of things' being as they are whether they are perceived or not. For that we need the idea of something that exists independently, not simply the idea of some feature present in our experience. Even if what we are aware of in perception are properties of certain kinds, and even if a property is thought of as an object of a certain kind, the enduring independent objects we believe in are not simply properties or collections of such perceived properties. Even a collection of properties can be thought of as an object, but that collection is not the object that those properties are properties of. To think or say of something that it has certain properties we need predication. And the object to which we ascribe properties in a predicational thought is something distinct from any or all of the properties we ascribe to it.

Thought of enduring objects therefore requires thought of something distinct from whatever properties we perceive and distinct from whatever fleeting perceptions we might be aware of. It requires the idea of the independent existence of an object: something that would exist and would be as it is whether it is perceived or not. Thought of an enduring object also seems to leave room for the thought that the object would be the thing it is even if some of its properties had been or will be different from what they are now. Modal ideas of dependence or independence are doubly present in such thoughts. We need those ideas even to think of an independent world of enduring objects at all.

Even the idea of *perceiving* what goes on in the independent world requires the idea of causal dependence. To perceive objects around us is to be affected by them in certain ways. And to understand that we perceive them is to understand that we would not perceive what we do if the objects were not there, and that if they are there and the conditions are right we are affected by them in certain distinctive ways. Thought of a world of independent, enduring objects with which we are in perceptual contact would be impossible without acceptance of the idea of the special modality involved in causal dependence.

This is a line of thought elaborated and defended with great delicacy by P. F. Strawson, following the lead of Kant. It is the idea of the causal or modal richness of the idea of an enduring object, and so of an independent world. Strawson focused on the essential links between our having a unified spatio-temporal system in which to place the enduring physical objects we perceive and think about and our thinking of those objects in what he calls the "weighty sense" of having certain causal or modal properties. In making sense of the world in the ways we do, our perception is not restricted only to certain qualities or sensory items. We perceive and have beliefs about enduring, independent objects. And:

> concepts of *objects* are always and necessarily compendia of causal law or law-likeness, [and] carry implications of causal power or dependence. Powers . . . passive liabilities, and dispositions generally . . . make up a great part of our concepts of any persisting and re-identifiable objective items.[5]

The thought of powers, dispositions, and liabilities involves the modal thought of causal dependence. And the upshot of Strawson's argument, like Kant's, is that "without some such concepts as these, no experience of an objective world is possible."[6] If that is right, trying to abandon the distinctive modality involved in causal or 'law-like' connections and get by with nothing more than correlations between perceived qualities alone would leave us with no intelligible experience and no thought of an independent world at all. The idea of causal or modal dependence is essential to such thought.

One reason many people have denied that we ever perceive causal connections is that they have thought there are no such connections in the world to be perceived. You cannot perceive what is not there. But this gets things backward for our purposes. We are looking for reasons for

---

5. P. F. Strawson, *The Bounds of Sense*, Methuen, London, 1966, pp. 145–146.
6. Ibid., p. 146.

denying that there are causal or necessary connections in the independent world in the first place. If epistemological considerations about perception and knowledge are to help support that conclusion they cannot rest on it.

One source of suspicion about the very intelligibility of the idea of causal dependence is that it cannot be expressed or defined in purely extensional terms which speak only of the actual occurrence or non-occurrence of objects or events of certain kinds. The idea of dependence appears to be irreducible to purely non-modal terms in which co-extensive predicates can be substituted one for another everywhere without altering the truth-value of what is said. I think the modal idea *is* irreducible to such purely extensional terms in that way. But that does not explain why that is felt to render the idea unintelligible, mysterious, or even problematic.

If we could somehow be reassured that everything that is so in the independent world must ultimately be expressible in such purely extensional terms, we would have good reason to think there is no causal dependence in independent reality. Anything not fully expressible in those terms could then be dismissed as confused or unintelligible. But to appeal to the exhaustive truth of an exclusively extensional description of the independent world in defense of a negative verdict about causation would be to appeal to one unsupported metaphysical prejudice to support another. I do not suggest that it is an unsupported prejudice that causal dependence cannot be adequately expressed in purely extensional terms. That is a debatable and more or less decidable claim of irreducibility. But in itself that claim carries no implications about the metaphysical status of the allegedly irreducible idea.

If the idea of causal dependence is in fact mysterious or unintelligible, one forthright response would be to simply abandon the idea in all serious thought about the world. That is what seemed possible for the idea of beauty; we could accept a metaphysical verdict to the effect that beauty lies only in the eye of the beholder and simply try to stop talking and thinking in ways that commit us to beauty as part of an independent world. We would then have to find other ways of saying and thinking what really matters to us about the objects we take that special interest in, and perhaps we could find a way to do that. But that does not seem possible in the case of causal dependence, which appears to play too deep and too pervasive a role in our thought of the world. The ways it appears fundamental and indispensable stand in the way of achieving metaphysical satisfaction by simply abandoning the idea altogether.

There has long been a philosophical picture of the general form of our conception of the world that encourages the thought that causation or any dependence involving that distinctive modality does not play an essential role. But I think this general picture has lasted as long as it has in philosophy only because it has not really been consistently adhered to and systematically applied. Philosophers have paid it a kind of intellectual lip service while surreptitiously continuing to think of the world in ways the picture itself cannot account for. I think restricting our thought within the limits of this impoverished conception would leave us unable to think in ways that are essential to our making sense of the world in the ways we do and unable to understand ourselves as having any reason to believe almost everything we believe about the world.

This more or less standard picture combines an attenuated version of the epistemology of Hume with the formal structure of first-order quantification theory. Everything that is so is to be expressed either in singular statements ascribing a predicate to an object—'Fa' or 'Gb' and so on—or in generalizations of the form 'For all x, if x is F then x is G' or 'For every x that is F there is a y that is G,' and so on. The predicates here pick out classes or kinds or properties of things, and the values of the variables are typically enduring perceivable objects, or perhaps events. This view therefore takes for granted that we perceive physical objects and can know by perception that they have certain properties. But it does not acknowledge the indispensability of the idea of causal dependence for thinking of enduring objects in those ways; on the contrary, its aim is to repudiate or otherwise explain away the distinctive idea of causal dependence.

The view holds in a Humean spirit that we can observe the occurrence or co-occurrence of individual objects of various kinds and general correlations between things of different kinds expressed in statistical or universally quantified generalizations. We can perceive that something of one kind occurs after something of another kind occurs, and we can come to recognize recurrent patterns of such conjunctions. But the most we could know by this kind of observation is that something of one kind sometimes or always happens after something of another kind happens.

If we were to ask *why* a particular thing happened, or why it happened when it did, the most we could appeal to, on this view, would be something else that happened earlier along with a generalization to the effect that things of that kind are sometimes or always followed by things of the kind we are interested in. But that would not necessarily explain why the thing in question happened. Such a universal generalization together with a statement of what happened earlier would *imply* that something of the second kind happened, but that would not explain it. If you *say* that such-and-such happened, what you say implies that it happened, but that does not explain why it happened.[7]

It would not be enough simply to add that an explanation must be more general than the particular fact to be explained. A generalization invoked to explain a particular fact is more general than the statement of what is to be explained, but it might still simply imply that the thing happened, without explaining it. Even if that generalization is implied in turn by higher-level generalizations about things of more general kinds, those more general truths still do not necessarily explain why the particular thing happened. They just say something more general from which the lower-level generalizations all follow.

It is true that in any effort to explain anything there comes a point at which something or other must simply be accepted as part of the way things are. In that sense, all explanation must stop somewhere. But with only higher- and higher-level generalizations or correlations to appeal to, there would be no explanation of anything. On this view, if Gs have always followed Fs in the past, and on a particular occasion an F now occurs without a G, we could 'explain' that non-occurrence only by appeal to the presence or absence on this occasion of something that was absent or present when every other G followed an F in the past. But with only actual correlations in the past to appeal to, there could very well be no such distinguishing factor at all. If a G did not happen after an F this time, and there is no such factor, there will simply be no explanation of that non-occurrence in anything that is true in such a world. All we could say was that what had been a universal correlation up to that point had simply broken down.

To think that such an unusual, singular event *could* not happen without something else in the world having been different, or to think that there *must* have been something different about the occasion in question to account for the non-occurrence of a G, is to invoke or at least to look for a dependence of one kind of thing on another. It draws on the idea that something of a certain kind simply *could not* happen unless something else were also so. But in a world of nothing more than correlated phenomena there would be no such dependences. We could not even think in terms of such dependences if we had abandoned as unintelligible the very idea of that distinctive modality. We could not seek an explanation of some surprising or so-far-unexplained occurrence on the

---

7. See Fred Dretske, "Laws of Nature," *Philosophy of Science* 1977.

grounds that there must be something that accounts for it. We could have no such thought.

Trying to make sense of the world in terms of nothing more than correlations between things of different kinds would also present us with the problem of which correlations in particular to pay attention to in getting expectations of what we think is going to happen next. We could not get our expectations on the basis of *all* the correlations there have been between things up to any given point. If that made any sense, it would give us indefinitely many conflicting expectations from the very same past occurrences. There are as many different correlations between members of the same kinds of things as there are different kinds to which those things belong. And there are as many different kinds to which the same things belong as there are different ways those things are similar to one another. So if *every* correlation were relevant to our expectations, the very same objects or events in the past would support to the same degree conflicting expectations about objects or events yet to be observed. This is the source of Nelson Goodman's 'new riddle of induction.'[8] It represents a deep challenge to any attempt to explain how we can have reason to believe something about the world on the basis of nothing more than correlations between objects or phenomena of different kinds.

A solution of this 'riddle' requires at the very least a distinction between correlations that do generate expectations of the kinds we actually get from our observations and all other correlations that in fact have no such effect on us. Certain distinctively 'well-behaved' kinds must be identified in terms of which we extend into the future what we take to be 'reliable' correlations we have observed in the past. It seems that no such distinction can be drawn solely in terms of actual correlations between things in the world. And to define the 'well-behaved' kinds as those that are invoked in causal or counterfactual or 'law-like' statements that allow us to infer something of the one kind from something of the other kind would be to make use of the special modality involved in causal dependence after all.

Any attempted solution to this problem in terms only of correlations between things would still leave us with nothing more than correlations. And the 'riddle' shows that with only correlations to go on we could have no reason to expect the correlations we had observed up to a given point to hold for any times or places beyond that. Very few neo-Humean

---

8. N. Goodman, *Fact, Fiction and Forecast*, Harvard University Press, Cambridge, Mass., 1955, ch. 3.

philosophers who share Hume's doubts about the idea of necessity or causal dependence would accept this epistemological point. They reject the distinctively modal idea, but they hold that, even without that modal idea, the observation of nothing more than correlations between things of different kinds can give us good reason to believe things about what has not yet been observed.

It was a mainstay of twentieth-century epistemology and philosophy of science that universal generalizations, understood purely extensionally, can be confirmed or supported by their observed instances. The fact that every F observed so far has been followed by a G was thought to confirm to some extent the general hypothesis that all Fs are followed by Gs. And as the positive instances accumulate, they were thought to give better and better reason to believe each time that the next observed F will be followed by a G. When this idea is taken strictly and held to consistently, I think it is clear that it cannot be correct. The mere accumulation of instances alone—if nothing else is known—gives us no reason in itself to believe a universal generalization that implies that all (or even the next, or the next few) still unobserved instances will follow the same pattern.

If, as the number of positive cases of a correlation between Fs and Gs increases, we believe there is getting to be better and better reason to expect the next F to be followed by a G, it cannot be simply because the number of Gs following Fs is increasing. It might well be true that we are getting better and better reason to believe the universal generalization, but if so it will be because the continuing correlation is increasingly good reason to think there is a connection of some kind between Fs and Gs: a relation of modal dependence between them.[9]

There being a connection or dependence between the two factors would explain why the correlation has been found to hold so far and why its holding so far is reason to expect a G after an F the next time. With no hint of a modal connection or dependence in the offing, a mere correlation alone, no matter how long it lasts, does not give us reason to believe such a thing. This is shown in completely general form from the structure of Goodman's 'new riddle of induction.' It is also borne out in everyday experience. Seeing more and more objects passing relentlessly along a conveyor belt and finding all of them so far to be red (or to cost less than $50), we do not thereby get better and better reason to believe that all objects still to come along the belt will be red (or will cost less

---

9. A convincing defense of this view, and much other good sense on these matters, can be found in Dretske, "Laws of Nature."

than \$50), or even that the next one will be, if we know or believe nothing involving any stronger or distinctive modality about what those objects are or where they come from or how they got there.

All this suggests that beliefs about causal or special modal dependences between things are indispensable to our thought of an independent world and to our understanding of how we could have any reason to believe anything about it. Even if that is true, it does not in itself imply that the world we think about in those indispensable ways is or must be the way we think it is. The indispensability does not directly imply that a metaphysical denial of the reality of causal dependence is not correct. This can be felt to leave the metaphysical question open. It can seem at least still possible to accept a negative metaphysical verdict about causal dependence while conceding that we simply cannot abandon all beliefs in such dependence on pain of having no thought of an independent world and no reasons to believe anything about it.

This is in effect the position of Hume. He would not deny that the idea of causal dependence is indispensable to our thinking of the world in the ways we do, and that without it we could have no conception of an enduring, independent world at all. But Hume regarded that as a fact about us and how we do and must think about the world, not a fact of the world we thereby think about. He held that the causal dependence we believe in is nothing in the world as it is independently of us and our responses to it. It is a certain kind of "fiction" we cannot help indulging in.

This shows that there is a way of understanding the indispensability of the modal idea of causal dependence according to which it does not imply that a negative metaphysical verdict about causation cannot be true. In that sense, the indispensability appears to leave open the metaphysical question of the status in reality of causal dependence. But there remains the different question whether or how we could find a negative metaphysical verdict about it *acceptable*.

We have seen that the acceptability of any metaphysical verdict depends on having an accurate account of the ways of thinking that are to be subjected to metaphysical assessment. I believe an accurate account of our thought about causal dependence would show that we regard the causal connections we believe in as holding independently of us and our responses to the world. We think the relations of dependence we believe in can hold between things independently of whether anyone thinks they hold or is aware of their holding or has any response to their holding or to anything else in the world. We think there were causal dependences between things in the world before there were any conscious beings to respond to them, and that there would have been such connections even if we had never been here, or even if there had never been any psychological responses by anyone to anything.

If all this is in fact part of what we believe in believing in causal connections between things, I think any reflection that would lead to a well-supported metaphysical verdict about causal dependence would have to concede that this is what we actually think. A negative metaphysical verdict says there are no such connections in the independent world. Since we believe that there are such connections, that metaphysical verdict would imply that the beliefs we hold to that effect are false or in some other way are not truly applicable to the independent world. That verdict might nonetheless be offered in a somewhat conciliatory spirit. One might grant that perhaps there are perfectly understandable reasons why we cannot help thinking of the world in that way. But the verdict still implies that we are wrong in those beliefs. In accepting the verdict we would see ourselves as victims of a certain kind of metaphysical illusion or error. The metaphysical reflections leading to that verdict would have revealed our error to us.

This is an outcome I think we cannot consistently reach. Trying to combine acceptance of a negative metaphysical verdict with acceptance of what I think is the correct account of our beliefs in causal dependence leads one into inconsistency, and in two different ways. To accept that we do believe that causal connections hold independently of us and our responses is to believe and take it to be true that there are such connections in the world. To agree that that is what we believe is to believe it. But the negative metaphysical verdict says that those beliefs about causation in the independent world are not true. So we cannot consistently believe both what this description of our actual thought says we believe and what the negative metaphysical verdict says about the truth of those beliefs. This is the first inconsistency.

This inconsistency would not arise if the beliefs we subject to metaphysical assessment were not our own. We can consistently accept a negative metaphysical verdict about the contents of beliefs we do not share, just as we can attribute to others beliefs we regard as false. It is only beliefs that we ourselves hold that we cannot consistently see as in error in that way. But it is our own ways of thinking of the world that we seek metaphysical illumination about. And if the contents of those beliefs conflict with what the negative metaphysical verdict says, we cannot consistently accept both.

Any attempt to support a negative metaphysical verdict would have to explain how and why we believe in independent causal connections even though there really are no such connections in the independent world. We would need a convincing explanation of our coming to the false beliefs we hold about causation. If some beliefs of that kind are indeed indispensable to our thought about a world, the explanation would have to explain why we cannot help getting beliefs of that kind. Putting it in very general terms, it would explain our coming to think in the ways we do as an effect both of what the world presents us with and of whatever is true of us that leads us to produce out of those materials our particular conception of how things are in the world. And it would have to explain how we do all this despite our never being presented in experience with any causal connections between things.

This is the second way this position would fall into inconsistency. Explaining our beliefs in this way would make essential use of the idea of causation or dependence. If we fully accept the negative metaphysical verdict that there are no such connections in the independent world we cannot consistently say that our beliefs in causation are the inevitable *effects* of what happens in our minds in combination with what the world presents us with. In accepting a negative verdict about causal dependence we cannot consistently offer causal explanations of our thought or of anything else in the world—at least not if the explanations are to be true of the world as it is independently of its being thought to be that way. The modal dependence invoked in an explanation of something cannot be any part of a world truly described by a negative metaphysical verdict about the reality of that modality.

This difficulty lies at the heart of the whole Humean program. Hume tried to avoid it by accepting causation when speaking or thinking as an ordinary person in the everyday affairs of life and denying it metaphysically as a philosopher engaged in abstract reflection in the isolation of his study. But that does not remove the inconsistency; it is only an attempt to avoid facing it.[10] The same person is present in both places and activities, and that one thinker cannot consistently accept both conclusions.

This second inconsistency might seem to be avoided by offering as an explanation no more than what a defender of a negative metaphysical verdict would be strictly allowed to say: not that the normal experiences of human beings inevitably *cause* them to believe that there are independent causal connections between things, but only that experiences of certain kinds are always in fact *followed* by those human beings' believing in causal connections between things. This is meant to be nothing

---

10. Hume does not succeed even in that, since in his philosophical reflections in his study he seeks answers to such questions as what "produces" or "gives rise to" our idea of necessity, or "what causes induce us to believe in the existence of body?"

more than an exceptionless correlation in human affairs. It is the most
that a defender of the negative metaphysical verdict could consistently
say by way of 'explaining' our beliefs in causal connections.

I raised doubts earlier about whether appeal to nothing more than
correlations between things could ever give us a satisfactory explanation
of anything. Those doubts apply with special force in this case. A certain
difficulty or embarrassment would arise in pursuing this particular
'explanatory' route to a negative metaphysical verdict. If there is even an
exceptionless uniformity in the way human experience leads us to
acquire our causal beliefs, then anyone who experiences successive
events of the appropriate kinds will in fact come to believe in independent causal connections between things after all. That is just what the
correlation implies. So anyone who undergoes the kinds of experiences
this 'explanation' says are the origin of causal beliefs will find himself
believing that there are independent causal connections in the world
anyway. If the person also accepts a negative metaphysical verdict that
says there are no such connections, he will still fall into inconsistency.
He could not consistently accept both the beliefs his 'explanation' says
we naturally acquire from our interactions with the world and a negative
verdict about the metaphysical status of those beliefs in reality.

The prospect of a conflict like this between believing in causation and
accepting a negative metaphysical verdict about the contents of those
beliefs is what makes some form of reductionism about those contents
continue to look attractive. If it could be shown that our apparently puzzling or problematic beliefs about causal dependence are really equivalent to something expressible in familiar and unproblematic non-modal
terms, there would be nothing extra or puzzling or mysterious in the
idea. It could perhaps even be defined by or reduced to nothing more
than observable correlations between phenomena of different kinds.

This is the source of the appeal of the so-called regularity analysis of
causation according to which two events are causally connected if and
only if one immediately precedes the other and both belong to classes all
the members of which occur in similar relations of precedence and sub-
sequence.[11] Understanding causal or 'law-like' connections in this way

11. Hume gives what he calls two "definitions" of 'cause.' The first, as a "philosophical relation," is "We may define a CAUSE to be 'An object precedent and contiguous to another, and where all the objects resembling the former are plac'd in like
relations of precedency and contiguity to those objects, that resemble the latter'"
(Hume, *Treatise*, p. 170). A "regularity" 'analysis' or reduction of causation would be
the upshot of taking this "definition" to express what we mean when we say or think

would support a negative metaphysical verdict about causation. That verdict arrived at in that way could no longer be expressed by saying that *there are* no causal or law-like connections in the independent world. On that reductionist view, there would be causal connections in the world, since there are correlations between things of the appropriate kinds, and causal connections are said to be nothing more than that. The verdict remains negative in denying positive metaphysical status to any distinctively modal connections between things.

"Regularity" reductionism of this form denies any distinction between correlations that 'just happen' to hold in the world and those that hold with a different or stronger modality. That is very hard to accept as an account of what we actually think. Recognition of some such distinction in our thought is just where reflection on the special character of our thought about causation began. We accept many things of the form 'Everything that is F is G' without granting that the corresponding modal statement 'If anything were F it would be G' is also true. We do not think everything of the form 'Every time an F happens a G happens' is equivalent to or implies 'Fs cause Gs' or 'Gs happen because Fs happen.' The problem we started from was to explain the difference between the two kinds of thoughts.

One thing that encourages the idea that the two ways of thinking must really be equivalent is the suspicion that any connection between things stronger than universal correlation is mysterious, or even unintelligible. We have so far found nothing to support that suspicion. But if there is anything in the suspicion, it would not be served by simply *equating* the two ways of thinking, as the "regularity" theory of the idea of causal dependence proposes. You cannot say that the whole idea of stronger causal or law-like connections between things is mysterious or unintelligible, and only conjunctions or correlations between things make sense, if you also think that all it means to say that there are causal or law-like connections is that there are such conjunctions or correlations.

Accepting the equivalence of apparently causal or law-like statements with universal generalizations would be to deny the very problem Hume thought he faced. In his search for the source of the idea of A as the cause of B, he found that an expectation of a B arises when every A observed so far has been followed by a B. But he thought that was not sufficient to

---

that two things are causally connected. I do not think Hume understands this "definition" in that way. In "defining" causation as a "philosophical relation" he means to state only what is so in the world when two things we regard as causally related are so related. It is in that sense a statement of a negative metaphysical verdict about the necessary connection or dependence we express in our thoughts about causation.

explain the appearance of the idea of causation. "There is a NECESSARY CONNEXION to be taken into consideration."[12] His problem was to explain how we get that idea of causal necessity even though we are never presented with instances of any such relation in experience. The explanation was meant to be consistent with a negative metaphysical verdict about causal necessity in the independent world.

In this last respect Hume agrees with what the imagined "regularity" theorist believes about the independent world; they agree on the metaphysics. But Hume sees something distinctive in our thoughts about causal dependence that is not captured by thoughts of mere correlations between things of different kinds. He thinks something new and distinctive happens in our minds when we observe things of two kinds constantly appearing together. Not only do we come to expect something of the second kind given something of the first kind; we expect it with a certain necessity or compulsion or unavoidability. To believe in causal dependence between things is to think of the world in a new and distinctive way that goes beyond the acceptance of mere correlations.

Hume thinks what leads us to get that new idea is an impression or feeling. If that is to be consistent with a negative metaphysical verdict about causal dependence, that impression or feeling cannot be understood as an impression or feeling *of* anything that is so in the independent world. It cannot be an impression of the necessity or dependence with which a billiard ball *must* move when struck by another, for instance. What then can be said about that 'impression of necessity'? What is it an impression of, and what can the idea of necessity that arises from it be said to be an idea of?

Hume never explained this in a satisfactory way, and it is perhaps easy to see why. He could not explain the idea of causal necessity by specifying some conditions in the world to which the idea would be truly applicable; he thought there are no such conditions. But our having that idea somehow makes a difference; we could not have causal thoughts without it. This means that what is special or distinctive about the idea of necessary connection can be only something special or distinctive about us. We who possess that idea come to respond to or think about the world in a new and distinctive way. But no conditions ever hold in the independent world in which what we think in that distinctive way is true. That makes it difficult to say anything helpful about what we think when we think in that new and distinctive way.

---

12. Ibid., p. 77.

One way of trying to understand this is to consider what happens in our minds when we get the idea of causal dependence. We might then take such psychological facts to be part of the very content of what we express in using that apparently modal idea in our causal beliefs. This too would be a form of reduction of the idea of causal dependence to something that involves no use of any special causal modality. On this kind of view, a statement of a causal connection between things of kinds A and B would not say simply 'All As are followed by Bs,' as on the "regularity" view, but something like 'All As are followed by Bs and everyone who observes an A comes with a feeling of necessity or compulsion to expect a B.'[13] To speak of causal connections between things in this way would be to say not only that a thing of one kind always follows a thing of another kind, but also something about human responses to things human beings observe. The truth of causal statements understood in this way would therefore depend in part on something true of us and our responses. This too would be a way of arriving at a negative metaphysical verdict about causation. Causal connections would not be any part of the world as it is fully independently of everything that is true of human beings and their responses.

This kind of view holds that there is explicit reference to actual observations and expectations of perceivers in the content of causal judgments. It therefore appears to imply that if no one actually observed things of two correlated kinds or had any expectation about them one way or the other, a statement of a causal connection between things of those kinds would not be true. That restricts the range of true causal statements to objects or events that have actually been observed by someone. But the scope of causation in the world is not so restricted, nor do we believe it is. We think causal connections hold even between things that human beings have never observed and never will observe.

---

13. This would be in effect to accept (a slightly altered version of) Hume's second "definition" of 'cause' as a "natural" relation as expressing what we mean when we say or think that two things are causally connected. "A CAUSE is an object precedent and contiguous to another, and so united with it, that the idea of the one determines the mind to form the idea of the other, and the impression of the one to form a more lively idea of the other" (ibid., p. 170). Hume's phrase 'determines the mind' would have to be replaced by something like 'is always followed in the mind' to eliminate a causal notion in favor of nothing more than regularities.

I do not think Hume means this "definition" to express what we mean when we say or think two things are causally connected either. Two things are "naturally" related when the thought of one of them naturally leads the mind to a thought of the other. Hume thinks causation is a "natural" relation in that sense, but he does not think that in saying that one thing causes another we say that it is such a relation.

This difficulty might seem easily overcome by holding instead that causal statements about unobserved objects say only that correlations between objects of those kinds *would* produce the relevant expectations if people *were* to observe them, or that people are *disposed* to get the relevant expectations from objects of certain kinds whether they have actually observed correlations between them or not. But this makes essential use of the very idea of counterfactual or law-like modality that was to have been explained. To say that such-and-such would happen if certain conditions were to obtain is to say something stronger than that such-and-such always does in fact happen. The idea of a disposition to regard or to respond to things in a certain way cannot be explained solely in terms of the responses people have actually had or will have to those things. Understanding our causal beliefs in those ways would not be consistent with accepting a general negative metaphysical verdict about causation.

Neo-Humean philosophers of the middle of the twentieth century faced similar difficulties in trying to do justice to the distinctive character of our thought about causal dependence while holding a negative metaphysical verdict about it. They did not focus, as Hume had done, on events that happen in our minds when we observe correlations between things, but on the distinctive way we think of some but not all of the correlations we observe and believe will continue into the future.

Those philosophers were right to insist that we do recognize a distinction in our thought between correlations or generalizations that just happen to hold or are only 'accidentally' true, and others that are 'nomic' or 'law-like' and appear to hold with a distinct and stronger modality. Ernest Nagel, for instance, observed that "No one seriously disputes the claim that a distinction something like the one baptized by the labels 'accidental' and 'nomic' universality is recognized in common speech and in practical action."[14] Richard Braithwaite held that

> it cannot be disputed that we do make a distinction of some sort between those empirical general propositions which we dignify with the name of "laws of nature" or "natural laws" and those which we call, sometimes derogatorily, "mere generalizations." A Humean philosopher may well deny that this distinction is one of objective fact; but if he denies that there is any distinction whatever, he runs counter to ordinary usages of language.[15]

---

14. Ernest Nagel, *The Structure of Science*, Harcourt, Brace, and World, New York, 1961, p. 52.

15. R. Braithwaite, *Scientific Explanation*, Harper, New York, 1960, p. 295.

Although we do think and speak in distinctively causal or law-like ways, those ways of thinking and speaking were not to be taken for granted as telling us how things really are. To regard the distinctive modality of 'nomic' generalizations as a *sui generis* and not further ana-lyzable aspect of the independent world, Nagel thought, would be to "postulate a property whose nature is essentially obscure."[16] Braithwaite held that to acquiesce in the idea of 'nomic necessity' "as a third ulti-mate category distinct both from logical necessity and from constant conjunction" would be to shirk one's duty as a philosopher, and to accept "something I know not what,"[17] something "transempirical in the world itself."[18]

These claims of obscurity in the idea of causal or 'nomic' connections appear to be based at least partly on epistemic considerations. In speaking of something "transempirical in the world itself" Braithwaite appears to mean something unknowable by empirical means, beyond the range of any experientially based knowledge of the world. Nagel too thinks that if there were something called 'physical' or 'real' necessity in the world it could be recognized only by some kind of "intuitive appre-hension."[19] If these charges of obscurity do rest on general epistemolog-ical doctrines, we have no more reason at this point to accept the obscurity or mystery of the idea of causal or law-like dependence than we have to believe the epistemological doctrines the charges appear to be based on. Those doctrines themselves are embedded in a conception of the world in which nothing more than correlations between things of different kinds is thought to be available. We have seen good reason to think that view cannot be convincingly defended and that our knowl-edge of the world cannot be adequately explained in those terms alone.[20]

Many followers of Hume have found the idea of causal dependence obscure or even unintelligible because they already accept a negative metaphysical verdict about it. If there is no such modality in the inde-pendent world, there is nothing in the world in terms of which the idea could be explained. That was the difficulty Hume faced in trying to explain the idea of necessary connection. In such a world, as Braith-waite puts it, there would be no difference in the "objective contents"[21] of what we think when we regard a generalization as 'nomic' and when

---

16. Nagel, *Structure of Science*, p. 52.
17. Braithwaite, *Scientific Explanation*, p. 294.
18. Ibid., p. 318.
19. Nagel, *Structure of Science*, pp. 52–53.
20. See above, pp. 26–31.
21. Braithwaite, *Scientific Explanation*, p. 295.

we regard it as 'accidental.' Under those conditions, to accept a distinct idea of causal or 'nomic' dependence would indeed be to accept something "essentially obscure," "something I know not what." With a negative metaphysical verdict already in place, nothing helpful would be left to say about the idea of causal dependence. But we are looking for reasons to accept such a negative verdict in the first place.

Whatever reasons those neo-Humean philosophers might have had for finding the idea of "objective" causal dependence obscure or mysterious, they thought they could explain our thought about it without themselves using that suspicious modal idea. The strategy was to show that the distinctive modality we apparently attribute to some but not all the correlations we believe in "does not reside in the objective relations of the events themselves. The necessity has its locus elsewhere."[22] The idea was that we "dignify" or elevate a universal generalization to the special status of 'law-like' or a law of nature only because of certain features of the generalization and its special position and function in the body of our thought about the world.

In order to succeed this strategy must identify the unique features of those generalizations we come to regard as 'law-like' and describe their special position and function in our thought. It must also identify the distinctive attitude we are said to take toward a generalization we regard as 'nomic' or 'law-like,' and explain what role our taking that attitude plays in what we believe in accepting a connection as causal or 'nomic.' And to support a negative metaphysical verdict about causation all this must be done without making essential use of the distinctive modality of causal dependence.

No account along these lines has succeeded in fulfilling all these requirements. On the first question, it was suggested that we accord the special status of 'law-like' to a generalization that is expressed in completely general, purely qualitative terms, is unrestricted in scope, holds true of many still-unobserved instances, and occupies a secure, high-level position in our knowledge of the world.[23] All this, it was thought, could be described in completely non-modal terms. But even if that were so, it would not be enough. Generalizations we recognize as 'accidental' and not law-like can also be found to satisfy the conditions so far specified.

---

22. Nagel, *Structure of Science*, p. 56.
23. A good account of the difficulties in picking out exclusively law-like generalizations by such descriptive criteria can be found in ibid., pp. 56–67.

Further discrimination appears to be found in the special function or role of generalizations we regard as law-like: they are said to serve to *explain* their instances or to *explain* the truth of the lower level generalizations that they imply, as merely 'accidental' correlations do not.[24] This grants the point I drew attention to earlier, that not every universal generalization explains its instances or explains what it implies.[25] But it leaves unanswered the question why some universal generalizations are thought to explain what they imply while others do not, even though on this view the "objective content" of every generalization is nothing more than a universal correlation between things of two kinds. The fact that we take a certain attitude toward some generalizations and not others (if we do) presumably does not in itself endow those generalizations with some explanatory power that is not possessed by other generalizations of exactly similar form to which we do not take that attitude.

Whether invoking a certain generalization could serve to explain something or not presumably depends on what the distinctive status we attribute to generalizations we regard as laws or law-like turns out to be. Does it help explain something by giving us a way to think of one thing as connected with or dependent on something else? We do appear to express some such connection in a counterfactual or subjunctive conditional: if an A were to happen a B would happen. On this strategy such conditionals are to be "explicated without employing irreducible modal notions" like physical or causal necessity.[26] Ernest Nagel accordingly suggested that what is asserted in a counterfactual or subjunctive conditional sentence is nothing more than that the indicative form of the consequent of the sentence ('a B happens') follows logically from the indicative form of the antecedent ('an A happens') in conjunction with a law of nature and certain other purely 'de facto' assumptions.[27]

This kind of view can be understood in different ways, but on each understanding it faces two serious difficulties. Even with a given law specified for the particular conditional statement in question, there is the formidable problem of determining which further 'de facto' assumptions can safely be added to the truth of the indicative antecedent to secure the implication of the consequent. Combined with one set of assumptions, the indicative consequent can be seen to follow from the specified law and the indicative antecedent; with the same law and

---

24. See, e.g., ibid., p. 63.
25. The difficulty of explaining anything in a world of nothing more than correlations between things was raised above, pp. 26–29.
26. Ibid., p. 56.
27. Ibid., pp. 71–72.

certain other equally de facto assumptions instead, it does not. As far as I know, there is no general solution to the problem of restricting the range of legitimate assumptions in a way that is consistent with the success of this neo-Humean strategy.[28]

But even if there were a solution to that problem, this strategy as it stands fails for another reason: it makes essential use of an unanalyzed idea of a law or law-like connection. A merely 'accidental' universal generalization can also be combined with the indicative form of the antecedent of a subjunctive conditional and some further assumptions to logically imply the indicative form of the consequent of that conditional. But that does not support or put us in a position to assert the subjunctive or law-like statement of connection between that antecedent and that consequent. The 'accidental' generalization 'All dogs born at sea are cocker spaniels' combined with the assumption 'This is a dog born at sea' implies 'This is a cocker spaniel.' But that does not imply, nor would we be in a position to assert on those grounds, that any dog born at sea would be a cocker spaniel, or that if this St. Bernard dog right before us had been born at sea it would have been a cocker spaniel.[29] Far from explaining the special modal idea of a law or law-like connection, this account makes essential use of it. It therefore cannot be used to support a negative metaphysical verdict about the special modality of causal or law-like connections.

But even if we had an adequate account of the origin or grounds of our accepting something as a law, there is a question about the role of that acceptance in our believing what we do about causal connections between things. Braithwaite describes belief in something as a law and not simply an 'accidental' generalization as a "belief in the truth of the [non-modal] generalization . . . accompanied by a belief about its origin."[30] When we assert something with what looks like the special modality 'If an A were to happen a B would happen' the sentence "refers to the origin of the asserter's belief" in the simple generalization that all As are followed by Bs.[31] And for those generalizations we regard as laws or 'law-like,' the 'origin' of our belief lies in their distinctive position or role in our theories or conception of the world. This view can be taken in at least two different ways. On one reading, it would mean that in

---

28. For an early but still convincing catalogue of the difficulties, and of their unavoidability, see Goodman, "The Problem of Counterfactual Conditionals," in his *Fact, Fiction and Forecast*, ch. 1.

29. An example from Dretske, "Laws of Nature."

30. Braithwaite, *Scientific Explanation*, p. 297.

31. Ibid., p. 299.

asserting something as a law or as law-like, the "certificate of origin" of our assertion—that the generalization occupies a certain position and has a certain function in our account of the world—would be part of what we assert. On this view, to say that something is a law, or in making what look like modal or law-like statements, we would be asserting in part something about ourselves and the state of our current body of beliefs. We saw that the same is true of the simpler reductionist parallel to Hume's "definition" of causation as a "natural" relation:[32] facts of what happens in human minds are part of what is asserted by all causal statements. That view was unacceptable for that reason. In this case, the idea that in asserting generalizations as laws or 'law-like' we say something about the "certificate of origin" of the generalization would have the same unfortunate consequence. Only statements that we accept and that have a certain distinctive role in our thought about the world would be causal statements or laws of nature.

This would mean that a particular modal or law-like sentence could be false when we assert it one day (the generalization involved is not part of our body of knowledge) and true when we assert it the next day (it now has a special role in our thought). It could be that the only thing that has changed in the interval is the state of our knowledge or the theories we accept. But in general we do not think that our believing something has any effect on what is or is not a law of nature, or on whether it is true that if an A were to happen a B would happen. We think many law-like statements are true of things we have never observed or even thought about; they hold independently of anything about us or the state of our thought or knowledge.

Furthermore, assertion is only one of many attitudes we can take to a causal or law-like statement. What can be asserted can also be considered or hypothesized or questioned or wondered about or denied. If what is asserted in a causal or law-like statement included something about the "certificate of origin" or the position or role a certain generalization in our theories of the world, that would also be what is considered or questioned or wondered about when we ask or wonder whether there is a causal or law-like connection between two things. But that is not so. To ask or wonder whether As cause Bs or whether a corresponding subjunctive conditional about As and Bs is true is not to ask or wonder whether a universal generalization about As and Bs occupies a certain special position in the body of our beliefs. The question is about the relation between one kind of thing's happening and another kind of

---

32. See above, pp. 37–38.

thing's happening, not about what is or is not part of our current theories of the world. It is perfectly intelligible to *suppose* that As cause Bs and that no relevant generalization concerning As and Bs is part of any theory anyone accepts. Since that supposition makes sense, a generalization's having a certain role in our current theories cannot be part of what we assert in asserting that As cause Bs or that if an A were to happen a B would happen.

As before, it would not help to try to avoid commitment to the actual state of our knowledge by saying instead that generalizations are regarded as laws or law-like if they *would* play a certain distinctive role in our thought if we were to accept them. Just as asking or wondering whether there is a causal or law-like connection between two things is not asking or wondering whether we *do* treat a certain generalization in a distinctive way, so it is not asking or wondering whether we *would* treat that generalization that way if it were part of our theories of the world either. But appeal to how we *would* treat certain statements is also to no avail for another reason. To speak of what we *would* do under certain non-actual conditions is to make essential use of the allegedly problematic idea of modal or counterfactual dependence. And to understand our causal beliefs in that way would not be consistent with accepting a negative metaphysical verdict about causal or law-like dependence in the world. That verdict says that what is so in the independent world is only everything that *is* so or *does* happen; not something that only *would* be so if certain conditions were fulfilled.

Braithwaite's suggestion that the "certificate of origin" of a universal generalization is involved in our assertion of something as causal or law-like could be taken in a different way that avoids these difficulties. It could be meant to draw attention not to *what* we assert when we assert something as a law but only to the conditions under which we assert the generalizations to which we accord that special status. If so, it would say only that we take a certain distinctive attitude toward generalizations that occupy a special position in our theories, but it would not imply that a generalization's having such a position in our theories is part of what we assert in asserting something as a 'law-like' or causal or subjunctive conditional statement. The role of the generalization in our thought would be relevant only to our *accepting* or *asserting* it as a law, but what we say or imply in such 'law-like' assertions would not be anything about us or our attitudes or the state of our theories.

This acknowledges the undeniable distinction between what is asserted and the conditions under which it is asserted. But to insist on that distinction in general, as it seems we must, means that a description of the conditions that must be fulfilled for asserting something does not necessarily tell us what we assert or believe in making that assertion under those conditions. In taking certain objects and events to be causally or modally connected we do take certain distinctive attitudes to them; we think of the objects and events as related to one another in a distinctive way, with a special modality. That is part of our accepting or believing in causal connections. But to specify only the conditions under which we come to have and assert those distinctive attitudes would not tell us what those attitudes are, or exactly what we accept or believe in accepting the causal connections we believe in.

That is what the metaphysical project must account for and explain. This neo-Humean strategy of focusing on the conditions of asserting something as a law does not explain it. Braithwaite concedes that on his view "it is impossible to say in general" exactly what is asserted in asserting that a universal generalization is a law or law-like. An "anti-Humean who demands a precise answer . . . [to this question] cannot properly be given one."[33] But the metaphysical project must give some account of our thoughts and beliefs about causal dependence. That is where it starts. Any attempt to unmask the distinctive content of those beliefs as not capturing anything that is so in the independent world must acknowledge and describe accurately the distinctive thoughts and beliefs we actually hold. The question is not simply under what conditions do we come to hold those beliefs. The question is *what* do we believe when we believe there is a causal or law-like connection between an A's happening and a B's happening.

This is what Hume saw he had to explain: what the 'idea of necessary connection' is, and how the use of it enables us to believe what we do about causal connections between things. He tried to explain what we believe by explaining how we come to believe what we do. We come to think of things in the world in a new, distinctive way as a result of reacting naturally to certain correlations or patterns in our experience. Since we never get an impression of a causal connection between objects, we "must draw the idea of it from what we feel internally in contemplating them.[34] Hume finds what he calls a "propensity" of the mind "to spread itself on external objects, and to conjoin with them any internal impressions, which

---

33. Ibid., p. 317. A precise answer cannot be given because according to the negative metaphysical verdict there are no conditions in the world in which the idea of a causal or 'law-like' connection between things would be truly applicable to something. See p. 36 above.

34. Hume, *Treatise*, p. 169.

they occasion, and which always make their appearance at the same time that these objects discover themselves to the senses."[35] By somehow "spreading" or "projecting" an "internal impression" onto external objects, we acquire a new and distinctive idea with which we can think of the world in ways we could not think of it before. We come to "gild or stain" the world with something derived from what we find only in our own experience,[36] and in that way we come to think of causal necessity as holding between the objects we perceive.

It is not easy to see how Hume thinks we manage to get these new thoughts from the impressions he thinks are available to us. I do not think the theory of impressions and ideas and nothing more than principles of association among them contains the resources to explain how thoughts and beliefs with causal modal contents are possible. This is a question of interpretation that I will not go into further.[37] What I think Hume cannot account for is our believing in causal connections that hold between things in the world independently of us and our responses. That is what he often says we do believe, and that is what I think he does not really explain.[38] The difficulty is to account for our holding beliefs we regard as true or false independently of whether we hold them or even have any responses to anything. That is what any appeal to 'projection' or 'spreading' of some internal response or feeling onto the independent world must account for if it acknowledges (as I think it must) that we actually think of the causal connections we believe in in those ways.

Simon Blackburn thinks this challenge can be met in a recognizably Humean spirit. He agrees that Hume does not say enough to make fully

---

35. Ibid., p. 167.

36. D. Hume, *Enquiries Concerning the Human Understanding and Concerning the Principles of Morals* (ed. L. A. Selby-Bigge), Oxford University Press, Oxford, 1975, p. 294.

37. I have described some of the difficulties in my *Hume*, Routledge and Kegan Paul, London, 1977, and in somewhat greater detail in my "'Gilding or Staining' the World with 'Sentiments' and 'Phantasms,'" *Hume Studies* 1993.

38. Hume also says "it is not possible for us to form the most distant idea of that quality, [a necessary connection between things] when it is not taken for the determination of the mind, to pass from the idea of an object to that of its usual attendant" (Hume, *Treatise*, p. 167). This suggests that we have no idea of independent causal connections at all; that in speaking of them as we do we refer to or invoke only our own responses. But with no intelligible idea of causal dependence there would be no beliefs in it, and therefore nothing for a process of "projecting" or "spreading" an idea on to the world to account for.

intelligible the "projection" of a full-fledged belief in independent causal connections from nothing more than "internal impressions." But he thinks the prospects of overcoming Hume's difficulty are bright. In the case of causation Hume was "working with exactly the same ingredients [as] in the case of ethics," and in ethics, Blackburn thinks, "it is much harder to believe that the problem is insoluble."[39] In fact Blackburn is more optimistic than that. He thinks "projective theories have everything going for them in ethics."[40]

The key for Blackburn is to understand that in making a transition from simply observing a succession of events to acquiring a capacity to make legitimate use of the richer vocabulary of causation we undergo what he calls a "functional" change. That change is not the mere arrival in the mind of a new mental item called 'an idea of causal necessity,' as Hume's theory of ideas would describe it. It is rather a new organization of the mind's activities and tendencies, brought about by observations of a mind naturally disposed to react to the world in certain ways.

In undergoing this change we thereby become capable of new ways of thinking and behaving that were not in our repertoire before, even of new attitudes toward some of the same objects or events we were aware of in more limited ways earlier. "Someone talking of cause is voicing a distinct mental set: he is by no means in the same state of mind as someone merely describing regular sequences,"[41] Blackburn says. In deeming a sequence to be causal we have undergone a "change in the structure of our thought." We have become masters of the activity of 'causalizing': thinking and acting and feeling in causal terms. But what we think in the terms we then use is not equivalent to or definable in terms of anything we could think earlier. "There is no way of . . . causalizing without using the vocabulary of cause, efficacy, or power."[42] And once we have made the transition:

> We think of the events as thickly connected, we become confident of the association, we talk of causation, and of course we act and plan in the light of that confidence.[43]

---

39. S. Blackburn, "Hume and Thick Connexions," in his *Essays in Quasi-Realism*, Oxford University Press, Oxford, 1993, p. 106.

40. Blackburn, "How to be an Ethical Anti-Realist," in *Essays in Quasi-Realism*, p. 178. In chapter 4 I consider how much projective theories have going for them even in ethics.

41. Blackburn, "Hume and Thick Connexions," p. 105.

42. Ibid., p. 105.

43. Ibid., p. 103.

We come to think not only

> that A causes B, but also . . . that there exist unknown causal connex-
> ions, that regardless of whether we had ever existed there would still
> have been causal connexions, and so on. We think in terms of causa-
> tion as an element of the external world.[44]

I think Blackburn is right to see the contents of the thoughts and
beliefs that are to be accounted for as true or false independently of us
and our responses. And I think he is right that the elaborate capacity for
'causalizing' that we acquire cannot be understood as a capacity for
thoughts whose contents are ultimately reducible to non-causal, non-
modal vocabulary. And there is no doubt that something very like what
Blackburn describes happens in our acquiring those irreducibly modal
causal beliefs. We start out in infancy with no thoughts of causal connections between things in the world at all; later, we have become
sophisticated 'causalizers.' And because of the irreducibility of the later
ideas there is no possibility of explaining our causal talk as simply a
new combination of ingredients that were available to us earlier. We
acquire a "distinct mental set." So both the beginning and the end of the
story Blackburn tells seem right.

But I do not think the kind of explanation he appears to offer of our
acquisition of that capacity overcomes the obstacles that defeat the more
strictly Humean view. To support the idea that those causal beliefs are
'projections' of some internal response onto a world that contains no such
connections, the account must say more than that we undergo a "functional" change from having no causal beliefs to believing in causal connections in the independent external world. It must also say something
about what that "functional" change amounts to: what is it a change from
and a change to, and how is that change brought about? Blackburn says
the "functional" change is "just like the onset of a passion" in being
"strictly nonrepresentative."[45] We start from responses that have no causal
modal content and are not perceptions of anything modal, and we eventually come to have thoughts and beliefs with distinctively causal contents
about an independent world. In doing so we acquire "a capacity to make
legitimate use of a term whose function is given nonrepresentatively."[46]

That is what an explanation in terms of 'projection' would seem to
require. But Blackburn does not tell us what those "nonrepresentational"

---

44. Ibid., p.105.
45. Ibid., p. 103. I take him to mean 'non-representational': it does not involve
representing things to be certain way.
46. Ibid., p. 105.

responses to the world he thinks we start from actually are, or what they are like. To give a "nonrepresentational" specification of the function of terms that eventually come to figure in the full causal vocabulary presumably involves describing the use of certain terms or the function of certain states without mentioning anything they refer to or any conditions under which what is said or thought would be true or false. To mention any such conditions would be to explain the terms or states "representationally." What is to be explained by the "functional change" Blackburn has in mind is how such terms or states of mind eventually come to occur essentially in thoughts and beliefs that we understand to be true or false of the world independently of our having the capacity for any such thoughts. I think what Blackburn rightly finds missing in Hume's explanation—"a link between the real functional difference and the thick content to give causal judgements"[47]—is still lacking in his own suggested account of 'projection.'

Blackburn defends what he calls a 'quasi-realist' view of causal dependence. That can make it look as if he wants to resist or at least not endorse what I am calling a negative metaphysical verdict about causation. He protests that it is wrong to think that his 'projectivist' account of our beliefs implies that in thinking in causal terms we make a mistake about the world; that "we make judgements with false contents."[48] According to his 'quasi-realist' account, we make no global mistake in our causal beliefs because, as he says, there *are* causal connections in the independent world. A negative metaphysical verdict says that 'There are necessary connections between things in the independent world' is not true. Blackburn says the only sense the 'quasi-realist' allows to the claim that 'there are necessities' is one in which it is true.[49]

I think all of us believe, with no metaphysical inclinations one way or the other, that there are necessary or causal connections between things. We believe it when we believe that a stone broke a window or one billiard ball made another ball move. The way Blackburn describes his 'quasi-realist' view makes it look as if the 'quasi-realist' simply believes in causal connections as all the rest of us do. But it is distinctive of 'quasi-realism' that it involves a 'projectivist' account of our beliefs about causation. If what the 'quasi-realist' believes were nothing more than what all the rest of us believe in believing in causation, there would be no difference between being a 'quasi-realist' who thinks we 'project'

---

47. Ibid., p. 104.
48. Blackburn, "Morals and Modals," in *Essays in Quasi-Realism*, p. 56.
49. Ibid., p. 57.

causal connections on to the world and simply believing what all of us believe about causation. 'Quasi-realism' and its associated 'projectivism' would collapse into nothing more than the view that there are independent causal connections in the world and we believe in them.

This threat arises from the very point or goal of Blackburn's 'quasi-realist' program. The task is to 'mimic' as closely as possible everything that could be said about causation by a metaphysical 'realist.' I take the 'realist' here to be someone who accepts what I would call a *positive* metaphysical verdict about causation. The metaphysical 'realist' says that there really are causal connections in the independent world. Blackburn thinks his 'quasi-realist' can say that too. He thinks the 'quasi-realist' can say everything that such a metaphysician would say to express his 'realism,' or at least can use all the same words as the 'realist' would use, but without expressing that 'realist' metaphysical view.

I think that is true. I think there is no form of words that uniquely and unequivocally expresses a metaphysical thesis about causation rather than something we all believe to be true or false of causation in the independent world. When we think and say what we do in causal terms we need not be saying anything of metaphysical significance one way or the other on the question of 'realism' versus 'anti-realism.' So if the 'quasi-realist' asserts nothing more than what all the rest of us believe and assert about causation, he would not necessarily be asserting metaphysical 'realism.' But would he be asserting anything distinctive called 'quasi-realism'? Not if he says and believes nothing more than what all the rest of us believe and assert.

Blackburn acknowledges this point when he observes that the success of the 'quasi-realist' program "would be a measure of the difficulty of defining a genuine debate between realism and its opponents."[50] It would be hard for a committed 'quasi-realist' to find anything to say that his alleged opponents would disagree with. That accords well with my own struggle here to identify the elusive issue thought to be at stake in a metaphysical 'debate' about the status in reality of this or that aspect of the world we think about. But if we can find no statable issue or question about 'realism' about causation, can we make any better sense of 'quasi-realism' or 'projectivism'? Is there a genuine debate we can understand between 'quasi-realism' and its opponents?

If what is involved in 'quasi-realist projectivism' is nothing more than explaining how we come to believe in independent causal connections

---

50. Blackburn, "Truth, Realism, and the Regulation of Theory," in *Essays in Quasi-Realism*, p. 15.

as we do, there would be nothing recognizably Humean about it. The 'quasi-realist' who can 'mimic' *all* "the intellectual practices supposedly definitive of realism"[51] could even say, as we would say, that people believe in causal connections because those connections are there in the world and they affect us in certain ways. The presence of such connected events right before our eyes is part of what explains our believing in them. This too expresses something I think we all believe. We see one billiard ball make another ball move, or we see someone push a door open. Seeing things like this can help explain why we think such things happen. But that explanation asserts that there are causal connections between things in the world. It is not recognizably Humean.

For Blackburn what is distinctive of his position is not what the 'quasi-realist' ends up saying—which is just what we all say and believe—but the way the view is arrived at in the first place. To become 'quasi-realists' he thinks we must start from an 'anti-realist' position about whatever subject-matter is in question and then eventually find a way to say everything that would be said in trying to express an opposed 'realist' view of that same subject-matter, without, of course, asserting metaphysical realism. Or at least he thinks we must "feel the anti-realist pull" about the subject-matter in question, or feel "squeamish" at first about "the existence of distinct states of affairs corresponding to our beliefs in these matters."[52] Without starting from such 'anti-realist' attitudes or inclinations there would be nothing distinctively 'projectivist' in what we end up saying and believing about causation. What the 'quasi-realist' says might sound like metaphysical causal realism, but it would say no more and no less than what the rest of us say.

This means it will not be easy for anyone who thinks he has succeeded in his 'quasi-realist' task to explain the appeal of the 'anti-realist' position from which he claims to have started. An 'anti-realist' about causation presumably says there are no causal connections in the independent world. And the 'successful' 'quasi-realist' says there are. How then could he explain what is or was attractive in 'anti-realism'? If the "anti-realist pull" is a pull toward the view that there are no causal connections in the independent world, how could someone who believes that there are such connections feel or express any force or pull from that 'anti-realist' view? Nor would it be easy for a 'quasi-realist' to say even in retrospect what he felt "squeamish" about. He was presumably not squeamish about engaging in the practice of 'causalizing'; that comes

---

51. Ibid., p. 15.
52. Ibid., p. 16.

easily to all of us. And if in engaging in that practice as he now does means he believes with complete conviction that there are causal connections between things in the world independently of us and our responses to them, how could he recognize or express the source of some alleged squeamishness he is said to have felt in speaking of "the existence of distinct states of affairs" "corresponding" to what he now believes about causal connections in the world? He is presumably not squeamish about believing that causal connections hold independently of whether he or anyone else believes in them. And he is not squeamish about saying that he and others believe in such connections. So he can unsqueamishly acknowledge that there are distinct states of affairs corresponding to what we all believe about causal connections; they are distinct in holding as they do whether anyone believes in them or not. In this way even the metaphysical-sounding vocabulary of 'realism,' with its 'distinct states of affairs' and 'correspondence,' can be 'mimicked' with no metaphysical implications.

Blackburn grants that his Humean 'quasi-realist' could go even so far in his 'mimicking' of the 'realist' position as to appeal to the presence of causal connections in the world to explain why we believe in them. "Once the mind has 'spread itself on the world,'" he says, "it also regards itself as reading things off the world it has projected."[53] It is perhaps not surprising that a mind that has 'projected' causal connections onto the world would then find them there, and even that it would then invoke them in explaining the finding of them. Although Blackburn admits that a 'quasi-realist' could give such a 'realist-mimicking' explanation, he thinks that is not the most "illuminating and economical" explanation for the 'quasi-realist' to give of our believing what we do about causation.[54] Blackburn thinks there is and must be a more fundamental or metaphysically more revealing explanation that does not 'mimic' anything a metaphysical 'realist' would say. It does not 'mimic' the denial of what a 'realist' would say either. The fundamental kind of explanation Blackburn thinks 'quasi-realism' depends on simply refrains from asserting anything causal one way or the other. As with Hume, there is to be "no explanatory role for any fact beyond that of regular succession in accounting for our opinion [of the existence of causal connections]; exposure to such succession, given natural propensities in the mind, is sufficient."[55]

---

53. Ibid., p. 32.
54. Ibid., p. 32.
55. Ibid., p. 31.

It is essential to 'quasi-realism' about causation that our believing in independent causal connections as we do can be adequately explained without having to suppose that there are any such connections in the world. Once we have causal beliefs, of course, we can also appeal to the presence of causal connections in the world to explain why we believe in them. But that is not the most "illuminating and economical" explanation the 'quasi-realist' can give of them. Once he has explained our causal beliefs in that causally non-committal way he can then go on to say and believe everything that sounds like metaphysical 'realism' but does not actually express it. And he will say nothing that even sounds as if it expresses 'anti-realism.' This is what makes it look as if the 'quasi-realist' does not endorse a negative metaphysical verdict about causation. The idea is that when he says those positive-sounding things that he and all the rest of us say and believe about causation he is not asserting any metaphysical doctrine about causation at all, any more than any of the rest of us are.

But believing in 'quasi-realism' must also be distinguished in some way from simply believing everything that all the rest of us say and believe about causation. What we all say and believe can sound like metaphysical 'realism' too, but it is not a metaphysical position at all. 'Quasi-realism' differs both from metaphysical 'realism' and from what all the rest of us say and believe. The difference lies in the 'projectivist's' commitment to what Blackburn calls the more "illuminating and economical" explanation of our having the causal beliefs we do. That explanation accords no explanatory role to causal connections in the independent world. The mind's 'projection' of the contents of causal beliefs produced from the non-modal materials the world presents us with is said to be sufficient in itself to explain our believing what we do. That is what creates the challenge I think both Hume's and Blackburn's versions of 'projectivism' do not meet; they do not give an intelligible account of that link. They do not explain how what they think we start with leads to the causal thoughts and beliefs we know we end up with.

We who believe in causal connections holding independently of us and our responses can accept that the presence of causal connections in the world is in part what leads us to believe in them. And we can acknowledge that in coming to have beliefs in causal connections in the first place we acquire a capacity for recognizing for the first time something that was there all along—causal connections. But that is not a recognizably Humean or 'projectionist' explanation of our acquisition of those beliefs. It says nothing of our 'projecting' causal connections on to a world that does not contain them. Blackburn's 'quasi-realist' explanation of the "functional" change that takes place in the mind is meant to be different from that. It says that when we make the transition to "a distinct mental set" involving the use of causal terms "no new aspect of the world is revealed by this change."[56] Something new happens in the minds that observe the successive events, but that change is not to be understood as a discovery of anything that is or was so in the independent world to which those minds respond.

That denial is essential to any recognizably Humean or 'projectivist' theory. Our causal beliefs are to be 'unmasked' as due to something about us and not to any causal connections that hold in the independent world. The goal of the 'projectivist' program as Blackburn describes it is to explain and even justify our use of a certain vocabulary "while denying that we represent a real aspect of the world to ourselves as we use it."[57] That denial is one thing that is meant to distinguish Blackburn's 'quasi-realism' from metaphysical 'realism' about causation. But that denial also represents a threat to the rest of us, who believe what we do about causation with no metaphysical implications one way or the other. How could we consistently accept it? How could we consistently say that beliefs we sincerely hold to be true do not represent a real aspect of the world we thereby believe in? Having undergone the "functional change" involved in acquiring the causal vocabulary, we use that new vocabulary to say how we think things are in the world we are presented with. We even use that same causal vocabulary in understanding how the world led us to acquire and understand those very terms in the first place. We recognize that in coming to think in causal terms we have learned something about how things are in the world. How then could we consistently agree that causal dependence is not a real aspect of the world we have come to believe in?

Denying that causal beliefs represent a real aspect of the world would present us with a further difficulty. We have seen that a belief in causation is presupposed in our understanding and recognition of many other familiar aspects of the world around us. How then can we even acknowledge a world of enduring objects that are as they are independently of our having any thoughts or beliefs about them if we agree that in thinking causally we do not represent any real aspect of the world? Blackburn acknowledges a difference here from what he regards as the more straightforward and unproblematic case of arriving at a negative metaphysical verdict in ethics:

---

56. Blackburn, "Hume and Thick Connexions," p. 103.
57. Ibid.

I do not think metaphysical obstacles stand in the way of the conception of nature that does the explanatory work in the example of ethics.
But many writers have difficulty with the conception of nature that is
supposed to do it in Hume's metaphysics of causation. Regularities—
but between what? Events—but how are these to be conceived, stripped
of the causal 'bit' . . . ? Events thought of as changes in ordinary objects
will scarcely do, for . . . ordinary objects are permeated with causal
powers. Nothing corresponds to the easy, sideways, naturalistic
perspective that strips the world of values.[58]

He does not explain how we can nonetheless accept a view that would
strip the world of all causation.

Such a conception of the world would be the result of explaining our
beliefs in causation on the general 'projectivist' strategy Blackburn has
in mind. When the process has done its work, he says,

we regard the world as richer or fuller through possessing properties
and things that are in fact mere projections of the mind's own reactions:
there is no reason for the world to contain a fact corresponding to any
given projection.
  So the world, on such a metaphysic, might be much thinner than
common sense supposes it.[59]

On the 'metaphysic' that the 'quasi-realist' accepts about causation,
the world is 'thinner' in some way than the 'richer' or 'fuller' world that
we who believe in causation believe in. It is 'thinner' in that the special
modal aspect of the vocabulary we use in speaking of causation does not
represent "a real aspect of the world." It is a "mere projection of the
mind's own reactions." And since causal connections are to have no
explanatory role in the 'quasi-realist' account of our coming to believe in
them, there would be "no reason for the world to contain a fact corresponding to any given" causal belief. This 'thinner metaphysic' therefore does ascribe to the claim 'there are necessities in the independent
world' a sense in which it is *not* true. Understood in the only way 'quasi-
realism' can be understood as a distinctive position, it must involve
some form of negative metaphysical verdict about causal modality as
part of the independent world. Otherwise 'quasi-realism' would say
only what all the rest of us ordinarily say and believe in our causal
beliefs, including our beliefs about the causal origins of those beliefs.

The 'quasi-realist' faces the difficulty of finding a way to state his 'metaphysic.' Using the very words we all use to express our causal beliefs, he

58. Blackburn, "How to Be an Ethical Anti-Realist," pp. 179–80.
59. Blackburn, "Opinions and Chances," in *Essays in Quasi-Realism*, p. 75.

could say the same as what all the rest of us say and believe about causation. There would seem to be no other words available to him. If he does somehow manage to state the 'thinner' metaphysical verdict that is definitive of his position, it looks as if what he says would be inconsistent with some of the things the rest of us say and believe about causation. It would even be inconsistent with what he himself says about the world in his everyday role as a 'causalizer.' Or at least his use of the *words* he uses to state his metaphysical position will be inconsistent with our use of the words we use to say what we believe about causation, and inconsistent with his own use of the words he uses in 'mimicking' metaphysical 'realism,' as all the rest of us also do.

In saying what we believe about causal connections between things we cannot consistently accept what the 'quasi-realist' says to express his metaphysics. If we understand what he says, we will insist to the contrary that with respect to causation the world is *not* 'thinner' than we thought. We find that it is just as 'rich' as we who believe in causation believe it to be, that causal dependence *is* a 'real aspect' of the world, that the world *does* 'contain the fact' that there are causal connections between things, and that it is *true* that there are necessities in the independent world. Of course, in saying such things we do not thereby assert metaphysical 'realism' about causation either. We could perhaps be said to be 'mimicking' it. But in fact we simply sum up in very general terms some of the things we believe about the world. We assert no metaphysical claim one way or the other.

If the 'quasi-realist' is to draw the metaphysical conclusion he thinks is warranted from the more 'illuminating and economical' explanations of our beliefs that he regards as fundamental, he must find a way to say or think or express that metaphysical conclusion. Otherwise, there will be no distinctively statable doctrine of 'quasi-realism' at all. But if the words he uses are used as all the rest of us use them, he will at some point deny things we all believe about causation. In this way the 'quasi-realist' must fall into the inconsistency I think is inevitably involved in accepting a negative metaphysical verdict about causation while believing in causal connections that are independent of us and our responses, as we all do.

Accepting a negative metaphysical verdict about causation also leads the 'quasi-realist' into the second kind of inconsistency we saw earlier. 'Quasi-realism' claims to explain how we come to believe in causal connections by appealing only to natural responses of minds like ours to a world that is not understood to contain any causal or modal connections. That raises again the question whether anything could ever be explained without some appeal to causal or modal dependence. To suppose that

the world has certain *effects* on minds that are naturally *disposed* in certain ways is still to make essential use of the distinctive idea of causal
modality. Dispositions must be understood modally, and effects must be
understood as more than events that merely succeed other events. I think
this second kind of inconsistency cannot be avoided by any version of
'projectivism'; the whole point of that theory is to give a causal explanation of our causal beliefs without holding that there is anything in the
independent world answering to their contents.

One could attempt in a Humean vein to avoid this second inconsistency by saying more cautiously only that everyone who is exposed to
regular sequences of events in fact comes to believe in causal connections. As we have seen, this would require a solution to 'the new riddle
of induction': since not all observations of regular sequences of events
are followed by beliefs in causal connections between things of those
kinds, the problem is to distinguish those that are from those that are
not. But even with that problem solved there would be nothing distinctively supportive of 'projectivism' in the idea that our getting beliefs
about causal connections is universally correlated with our observing
certain sorts of correlations between those kinds of things.

Someone could accept that general correlation and then go on to
explain why it holds. One explanation could be that the events we
observe are correlated as we find them to be because they are causally
connected with one another, and that it is because we take them to be so
connected that we are led to believe in causal connections as we do.
That explanation accepts all the mere correlations that the 'quasi-realist'
would appeal to, but it says more. And accepting that fuller explanation
is not consistent with a 'projectivist' account of the origin of our beliefs.
A 'projectivist quasi-realism' that says there is no 'more' to appeal to—
that there are only the correlations between our observing the events and
our coming to believe in causation—thereby accepts a negative metaphysical verdict about causation.

I think the conclusion is inescapable: understanding ourselves as
believing in causal connections holding fully independently of us
and our having the responses we do is inconsistent with accepting a
negative metaphysical verdict about causation. And I think we do
regard the causal connections we believe in as independent of us in
that way; no reductionist account that would eliminate the modal element
is acceptable. So we cannot accept a negative metaphysical verdict
about causal dependence and consistently continue to accept all the
things we believe involving causal modal connections between things
in the world.

This is so far a purely negative outcome. It says only that we cannot consistently carry out a task that is meant to lead us to a certain conclusion. For that reason alone it can be less than fully satisfying. It seems to offer nothing positive in the face of what is thought to be a pressing metaphysical problem. We start out wanting to hold our whole way of thinking up to a certain kind of critical scrutiny without simply going along with it or taking it at face value. We want to understand exactly what our thoughts of causal dependence amount to, and whether they capture something that is really so in the world independent of us. To say only that we cannot consistently accept a negative answer and leave it at that can look like simple acquiescence in our everyday beliefs with no further explanation of that distinctively causal way of thinking.

But to acknowledge the irreducibility of the terms of the causal vocabulary and grant, or even insist on, the unacceptability of a negative metaphysical verdict about causation is not necessarily simply to acquiesce in our current 'causalizing' or to refuse to subject it to further philosophical scrutiny. We can continue to try to understand more clearly what our capacity to think and act in causal modal terms enables us to do that we could not do without it. We can increasingly reveal the complexity of that distinctive way of thinking and explore the degree of its indispensability and its sources. That is just what responding to the metaphysical project in the ways I have been pursuing encourages us to continue to do. We can come to understand better and better what our causal thought amounts to.

I know that even at its best this kind of philosophical exploration can be found metaphysically unsatisfying. It is and aspires to be a description of our ways of thinking, but as nothing more than a description it can still feel like ungrounded and therefore uncritical acquiescence in an admittedly complex body of beliefs and attitudes without offering any deeper metaphysical understanding of their relation to the reality they purport to be about. This is a very familiar form of philosophical disappointment or dissatisfaction. It is difficult to know what to do in the face of it. It can lead us to continue searching for an understanding of our causal judgments that either gives us the kind of reassurance we seek or shows them to be no more than distinctive responses on our part to what a modal-free independent world presents us with. But if pressing on for an understanding that we can eventually find satisfying leads to distortion of what we actually think about causation, we will avoid frustration and metaphysical disappointment only at the cost of misunderstanding ourselves.

3

Necessity

Everything that is red and round is round. The sum of seven and five is twelve. If one stick is longer than another and the second is longer than a third, then the first stick is longer than the third. Not only are these and many other sentences like them true; what they say could not possibly be or have been false. Their truth holds with necessity, just as their denials could not possibly be true. Not everything that holds with necessity is as obvious and apparently trivial as these elementary examples. The necessity with which something holds is therefore not to be identified with its obviousness or apparent triviality. Nor is something's holding with necessity the same as its being known to be true or known to be false. There are many statements that are not known to be true or known to be false whose truth-value could not possibly have been different from what it is. And there are many statements that hold with necessity without being known to hold with necessity.

What is distinctive of all these truths and falsehoods is their special modality: the *way* they are true or false. They have their truth-values necessarily, with no possibility of things' having been otherwise. This kind of necessity is stronger than that of laws of nature or counterfactual or subjunctive conditionals. Statements of those kinds can be said to express how things *must* be, but the necessity or dependence expressed in that distinctive modality seems still in an absolute sense contingent. As things are, unsupported bodies in a gravitational field must fall at such-and-such a rate, but it seems at least possible for things to have been otherwise in that respect. There might have been other ways things had to behave. But it is not possible at all for things to have been otherwise where this stronger form of necessity is concerned. It appears to be absolute and to depend on nothing that could have been otherwise.

This stronger idea of certain things' holding necessarily, with no possibility of having been otherwise, makes its appearance in different ways and at different places in our thought. The simplest and most straightforward application of the idea is in thinking that something or other is true and holds necessarily. If it is necessarily true that p it could not possibly have been false that p. I will concentrate here on this basic idea of necessity and possibility as ways or 'modes' in which something can be true or false. I think that fundamental idea alone gives us enough to raise the most general metaphysical question about its status in reality. The presence of any 'absolute' necessity at all in the world as it is independently of us is what is thought to be metaphysically problematic.

There are many statements of very simple and transparent form that we have no difficulty recognizing to be true (or false) with no possibility of their having had a different truth-value. I do not mean to suggest that it is always easy to tell whether something holds necessarily or not. On the contrary; we have no firm conception of the scope of all those things that hold necessarily, and no effective procedure for determining whether any random candidate falls within it. But that casts no doubt on whether it is necessarily true that everything that is red and round is round, for instance, or on a great many other equally obvious cases. Since what is in question here is not the extension of the class of necessary truths but the metaphysical status of the necessity we unhesitatingly attribute to some truths we take to have that special modality, I think we can proceed with simple, uncontroversial examples we all recognize as holding necessarily.

One centrally important application of the idea of necessary truth is in the necessity with which the truth of one statement requires and so implies the truth of another. That link is essential to the possibility of valid inference and proof. It is only because we can see that a certain thing must be true if a certain other thing is true that we can move in thought with no possibility of falsehood from one thought to another. In the same way, we can recognize inescapable incompatibilities: that if a certain thing is true certain other things could not possibly be true. Accepting that some things hold with this kind of what looks like 'absolute' necessity appears to be pervasive in our thinking and indispensable to any determinate, structured inquiry.

Without denying that we do or even must think in these ways, it is possible to find this necessity puzzling or mysterious in relation to a reality that is thought to be independent of its being thought of in this or that way. It is easy to feel that we cannot simply take this apparently absolute necessity for granted as part of the way things are. We would like to "explain" or "ground" it in something or other, or "get behind" it in some way that accounts for its metaphysical status and makes it intelligible to ourselves as part of the world. But could there be any such necessity in the world as it is completely independently of us and all our ways of thinking of it? That independent world would then include not only everything that is in fact so but also everything that absolutely must be so as well. But how could certain things absolutely *have* to be so in the world as it is completely independently of us and our thoughts about it? A satisfyingly positive answer to this metaphysical question can seem unreachable.

The challenge seems even greater here than with causal necessity or modality. Perhaps it might finally have to be accepted that objects in the independent world stand in relations of causal dependence to one another—that that is simply part of the nature of those objects, as it were—even though the world could have been different from what it is. But can we understand how absolute necessities and possibilities could simply hold in the nature of things? In the nature of *what* things? With that kind of necessity there seems to be no possibility of things' being or having been otherwise at all. Something's holding necessarily in that sense does not appear to depend on anything. Or if it does depend on something else in some way, does that mean that the familiar necessities we accept are not really absolute after all? But then what could they depend on? And what kind of dependence could that be?

One source of metaphysical resistance to causal or law-like dependence as part of the world was epistemological. If there were such connections in the world, how could we ever know or have reason to believe in them on the basis of what the world presents us with? But the epistemological doctrines that encourage unmasking causal beliefs as somehow due only to us and our responses were found less than compelling in that case. Epistemological assumptions have also played a role in encouraging a similar metaphysical unmasking of absolute necessity. They appear to put constraints not only on the possibility of knowledge of necessity but on the very understanding of necessity itself.

One venerable epistemological doctrine has long dominated this subject: that we cannot know something to be necessarily true on the basis of experience, or that all knowledge of necessity must be a priori. This view has a long history, going back in one form or another at least to Plato. It was central to Leibniz and Kant and to many more recent defenders of a priori knowledge. Even philosophers who deny that we know anything a priori appear to accept the doctrine. John Stuart Mill thought arithmetic is known on the basis of experience, and so felt constrained to deny that its truths are absolutely necessary.[1] Quine held that none of our beliefs is completely immune to revision at the tribunal of experience, and partly for that reason rejected the notion of necessary truth completely.[2] Both appear to share the assumption that if something is known to be necessarily true it cannot be known on the basis of experience.

The doctrine is found in its most explicit form in Kant:

> Experience teaches us that a thing is so and so, but not that it cannot be otherwise. [So] if we have a proposition which in being thought is thought as *necessary*, it is an *a priori* judgment.[3]

'*A priori*' here is an adjective true of knowledge or a way of knowing that is completely independent of all sense experience. This offers what Kant calls a "sure criterion" or "secure indication" of the a priori in the sense that the necessity or 'strict universality' of the proposition claimed to be known is enough to determine that if it is known it is known a priori and not by experience.[4]

This doctrine is not easy to explain, let alone defend. A priori knowledge is knowledge independent of all experience. But it has proved difficult to specify the legitimate range of 'experience' as it bears on one's knowledge of the world. And it must be explained how one's knowledge of something can be 'completely independent' of one's knowledge of something else, and so independent of one's experience. Any explanation must rely on some fairly definite conception of what *can* be known on the basis of experience and of how that knowledge is possible. Some conception of the limits of what *can* be known on the basis of experience obviously lies behind Kant's taking necessity to be a 'criterion' of something's being known independently of experience. He says, for instance:

> experience never confers on its judgments true or strict, but only assumed and comparative *universality*, through induction. We can properly only say, therefore, that so far as we have hitherto observed, there is no exception to this or that rule. . . . Empirical universality is only an arbitrary extension of a validity holding in most cases to one which holds in all, for instance, in the proposition 'All bodies are heavy.'[5]

---

1. J. S. Mill, *A System of Logic*, Longmans, Green, London, 1956, book 3, ch. 24.

2. See e.g., W. V. Quine, "Two Dogmas of Empiricism," in his *From a Logical Point of View*, Harvard University Press, Cambridge, Mass., 1953.

3. Kant, *Critique of Pure Reason* (tr. N. Kemp Smith), Macmillan, London, 1953, B3, p. 43. For fundamental objections to this 'criterion,' with far-reaching implications, see S. Kripke, *Naming and Necessity*, Blackwell, Oxford, 1972.

4. Kant, *Critique of Pure Reason*, B4, p. 44. I take 'strict universality' to be the necessity of a universal generalization.

5. Ibid.

This implies not only that necessary truths cannot be known on the basis of experience, but that even contingent universal generalizations cannot be known by experience either, if any of their instances remain unexamined. If experience can give us knowledge only of what has been observed to hold without exception so far, and the most we can do is "arbitrarily" extend any correlation we have observed to all future instances, we could never know or have reason to believe anything about any instances still to come. Or if we could know it, we would have to know it a priori.

This view of the limits of empirical knowledge also implies that we never know by experience of any causal or modal connections we believe to hold between things, since these too go beyond correlations all of whose instances have been observed. If the causal or modal connections we believe in are in an 'absolute' sense still contingent, and things could have been otherwise in certain ways, we believe what we do about causal connections in the world because of the experience we have of the actual world in which we find those connections to hold. Of course we do not come to believe in causal connections between things by inferring them directly from any mere correlations we observe. The modal idea of causal dependence is a new and richer idea we come to apply to the world in the course of making sense of it. Learning when and why that idea applies in particular cases is a complex capacity that involves much more than merely recognizing correlations. But that does not mean that our knowingly applying that idea to something is not based on experience.

The more restricted one's conception of the kind of knowledge we can get through experience, the more plausible it will seem that many of the things we know are known independently of experience. But the restrictions must not be so severe as to leave us knowing virtually nothing that we now think we know on the basis of experience. That would give us more reason to reject the proposed 'criterion' of the a priori than to conclude that we do not know such things at all, or that if we know them we know them a priori. It remains to be seen whether necessity can be defended as a 'criterion' of the a priori on a more tolerant and so more realistic conception of how we actually come to know the things we know on the basis of experience.

I will not pursue that epistemological question. What matters for our purposes here is the way this epistemological doctrine of the a priori character of our knowledge of necessity imposes constraints on the metaphysical investigation of the status of necessity itself. The influence is indirect, but deep. Along with other assumptions, it can make an overwhelmingly strong case for a negative metaphysical verdict about what would otherwise be the inexplicable necessities and possibilities we believe in.

If the necessities we know were part of the world as it is independently of us and our responses to it, and if all necessary truth is knowable only a priori, some explanation would be needed of how we can have a priori access to those ways the independent world must be. It has been widely argued that this is something we cannot have. That is a lesson we are said to have learned from the history of traditional metaphysics—perhaps the only solid thing to be gained from that sad history. The idea is that there can be no a priori insight into how things are or must be in a world completely independent of us. We have no conception of any quasi-perceptual but still a priori intellectual 'vision' of such a world, or of any mechanisms that could provide information about such necessities in the way sense perception puts us in touch with a world of independent contingent facts. If we nonetheless believe that we know many things to be necessarily true, which seems undeniable, and Kant's 'criterion' implies that we know them a priori, those necessities and our a priori knowledge of them would have to be accounted for without invoking any independent world or any a priori access to such a world. Accepting these epistemological constraints on our knowledge of necessary truth can seem to leave no alternative to accepting a negative metaphysical verdict about necessity.

The key to understanding necessary truth and a priori knowledge in this metaphysical way has most often been expressed in the idea that all necessary propositions are 'analytic': true or false solely in virtue of the meanings or contents of their constituent concepts and the relations among them. The idea is that anyone who can think at all must have concepts and so can know the corresponding necessities that express the contents of those concepts or the relations among them. And since those necessities are known from an understanding of the concepts alone, the knowledge is said to be independent of all sense experience and so a priori. It is knowledge only of what is already 'contained' in one's concepts.

Whether this can explain necessity and our knowledge of it in a way that sustains a negative metaphysical verdict about necessity depends on exactly how this doctrine of the 'analyticity' of necessary truth is to be understood. As I have presented it so far, I think it does not offer either the epistemological or the metaphysical satisfaction we seek. Epistemologically, it does not explain how possession or understanding of a concept can provide knowledge of the truth of something, and how that knowledge can be independent of all experience. Metaphysically, it does not help explain the nature or status of the necessities and possibilities we believe in and think we know.

One indication that something more is needed is that the doctrine as described so far could be accepted even by someone who believes in a domain of concepts or properties or universals or other abstract objects standing in certain fixed relations to one another in a world completely independently of us and our responses. The necessary truths we know could then be said to be true solely 'in virtue of' the contents of and relations among those concepts or properties or universals. Since anyone who can think must have concepts, and so must be capable of knowing some necessary truths, 'access' to or knowledge of those truths could be said to be by thought alone. Thinking of concepts and the relations among them in this way would be compatible with holding that all necessary truths are analytic in the sense explained so far.

This position is unsatisfactory epistemologically, on the so-far unquestioned assumption that we can have no a priori insight into a domain of independently existing concepts or properties and the necessary relations among them. It does not explain how knowledge of the necessary truths we know we have is possible. This view is also dissatisfying metaphysically. It appeals to concepts and the relations among their contents, but the modal vocabulary of necessities and possibilities is needed even to understand such talk. One concept differs from another if it is *possible* for the one to be true of something while the other is not. One concept is said to 'contain' another if, given that the concept is true of something, the other *must* also be true of it. To speak of concepts and the relations among them in this way without further elaboration would be to acquiesce in unexplained acceptance of necessities and possibilities. The '*must*'s that serve to identify concepts and the relations among them express some of the modal truths that the appeal to the 'analytic' character of all necessities was meant to explain. We make no metaphysical progress by appealing to something the possession or understanding of which involves unexplained acceptance of necessities and possibilities that we want to account for.

This is perhaps only to be expected if the modal vocabulary of necessities and possibilities as we understand it is irreducible to any set of equivalent but non-modal terms. This is how it seems to be. There is an equivalence between something's being necessarily so and its not being possible for it not to be so, but that makes use of one modal notion in explaining another. It provides no independent understanding of all the modal relations we believe in. The general irreducibility of the modal vocabulary to something that does not presuppose it seems to leave no prospect of explaining necessity by any combination of non-modal facts that somehow "make" necessary truths true, or "in virtue of which" they are true. And any equivalence that could serve to express some such reduction would itself have to be understood to hold necessarily. Citing necessities or possibilities in an attempt to explain the necessity or possibility of something takes for granted the very necessity we want to understand. Appeal to an independent world of concepts and properties and the necessary relations among them therefore provides no metaphysical satisfaction about the nature or status of necessity.

The real metaphysical and epistemological promise behind the appeal to analyticity was that it would explain at one stroke both the nature of the necessities we believe in and our a priori knowledge of them. These are different goals, to be achieved in different ways, and the differences between them have not always been clearly recognized or acknowledged. Nor has the difficulty of achieving both these goals at the same time, and with one and the same idea. That is perhaps one reason why efforts to explain the doctrine of the analyticity of all necessary truth have rarely been found fully satisfactory. Too many competing demands seem to have been placed on a single notion; the idea of analyticity was probably expected to do too many things at once.

The full promise of the appeal to analyticity can be fulfilled only if necessary statements that are true or false solely in virtue of the relations among concepts or meaning alone can be understood to describe or state nothing that is so in any world independent of us and our ways of thinking of the world. The thought is that if necessary truths say nothing about the world at all, and are not "made" true by or "in virtue of" anything that is so in any independent world, then no special epistemic access to such a world would be needed to explain our a priori knowledge of them.

When the doctrine of the analyticity of necessary truth is understood to carry these richer implications it becomes an expression of what I call a negative metaphysical verdict about necessity. It acknowledges that we do know many things to be necessarily true, and that we know them a priori, but it says that there is no such thing as the necessity we apparently believe in in any world as it is fully independently of us. The necessity and our knowledge of it are to be fully accounted for only in terms of something that is true of us and our ways of thinking about the world. What is intended is an unmasking that is parallel in form to a negative metaphysical verdict about causal dependence. There is to be nothing corresponding to the apparently distinctive modality of such beliefs in the world as it is independently of our thinking of or responding to it in the ways we do. The two verdicts about the two different kinds of modality belong to the same metaphysical genre as the idea that beauty lies only in the eye of the beholder.

It is not easy to understand, or even to express, the idea that in saying something that is necessarily true necessary truths say nothing about the world. One way to try to express it is in terms of the "emptiness" or "non-factual" or "purely formal" character of necessary truths. Carnap said "logical statements [that] are true under all conceivable circumstances . . . do not say anything about the world."[6] Not only can they "be established without any regard to the facts," they "do not convey any information about facts; this is sometimes formulated by saying that . . . [they have] no factual content."[7] They are "sentences of a different, non-factual kind. . . . If we call them true, then another kind of truth is meant, one not dependent on facts."[8] They do not "say anything about the facts of the world."[9]

This as it stands is puzzling. Each necessary truth says *something*, and what it says is different from what each of the others says. Every sentence that is true can be said to state a fact—something that is so. So how could a necessary truth, which states something that must be so, fail to state a fact, even a fact of the world? If what we mean by 'the world' is everything that is so—everything that is the case—then what is said by the sentences 'Everything that is red and round is round' or 'The sum of seven and five is twelve,' will be facts of the world in that sense. They are facts that could not possibly have been otherwise. What is the conception of a 'world' and of 'facts' according to which such statements say nothing about the world and state no facts? Whatever conception of 'the world' that might be, it is different from the idea of the world as everything that is the case—what is said to be so by everything that is true. Perhaps what is at work is a conception of a metaphysically 'purified' world in which only some but not all of the things we take to be true are really true. But how is such an 'improved' view of the world as containing no necessity to be arrived at in the first place?

Of course, to say that necessary truths do not state facts of the world might just mean that they do not state facts of what has come to be called the 'empirical' world. That is to say that they do not state facts that can be known 'empirically.' We saw that the questionable assumption on which this whole line of thinking appears to be based is that necessary

6. R. Carnap, "Intellectual Autobiography," in P. A. Schilpp (ed.), *The Philosophy of Rudolf Carnap*, La Salle, Ill., 1963, p. 25.

7. R. Carnap, *Foundations of Logic and Mathematics*, University of Chicago Press, Chicago, 1939, p. 15.

8. Ibid., p. 2.

9. Carnap, "Intellectual Biography," p. 46.

truths can be known only a priori, not empirically. But even if that is true it does not imply that those truths state no facts of the world. It says only that they do not state facts that can be known in a certain way.

To say that necessary truths do not state facts of the world might mean that they do not state facts of the contingent world of what happens to be true but could possibly have been otherwise. This seems to be how Carnap thought of them. He sometimes calls a truth 'factual' only if it is neither necessarily true nor necessarily false.[10] But to say that necessary truths are not factual in that sense is only to say that they are not contingent; they do not state facts that could possibly have been otherwise. That is true, but it does not imply that they do not state *any* facts at all or do not say *anything* factual. They hold necessarily, so they could be said to state necessary facts of the world or to have necessary factual content.

It might be protested that there is no such thing as 'necessary facts of the world' or 'necessary factual content': that something is a fact only if it is at least possible for it to have been otherwise. Analytic necessary truths do not state anything that could even possibly have been false. They could therefore be said to be "empty" or "devoid of factual content" in the sense that they do not rule out or rule in as actual any of the ways things are that could have been otherwise. But that does not imply that a necessary truth says *nothing* about the world. What it says is something that could not possibly have been false, and so is compatible with every genuine possibility.

Resistance to this idea is sometimes put by saying that necessary truths "tell us" nothing or "convey no information" about the world. Wittgenstein said that in knowing 'Either it is raining or it is not raining' I know "nothing about the weather."[11] Ayer said that the sentence 'Either some ants are parasitic or none are' "provides no information whatsoever about the behaviour of ants, or, indeed, of any matter of fact."[12] It must be granted that in knowing the truth of Wittgenstein's sentence I do not know anything that will help me decide whether or not to take an umbrella. It gives no information as to which of its two disjuncts is true; nor does Ayer's sentence about ants. But each sentence says, and in that sense provides the information, that either one or the other of its disjuncts is true. Ayer observes that that is "information we already have"; necessary truths, he says, "add nothing to our knowledge, for they tell us

---

10. E.g., Carnap, *Foundations of Logic and Mathematics*, p. 13.

11. L. Wittgenstein, *Tractatus Logico-Philosophicus* (tr. D. Pears and B. McGuinness), Routledge and Kegan Paul, London, 1961, 4.461.

12. A. J. Ayer, *Language, Truth and Logic*, Dover, New York, ... n.d., pp. 78–79.

only what we may be said to know already."[13] But if they tell us only something we know already, they must tell us something. It must be admitted that many necessary truths tell us nothing we did not know already, but the same can be said of many contingent truths as well. There are many things that are known by anyone who knows anything. That does not mean they say or tell us nothing about the world.

But in fact it is not true that all necessary truths say or tell us only something that everybody already knows. Many necessary truths say something that nobody knows; some even say something that nobody will ever know to be true. To say they 'tell' us something or convey certain 'information' is not to say that we can come to *know* or even believe what they say or tell us just by hearing them or thinking about them. We are often not in a position to recognize the truth of what such statements say even when they are true. But that is a fact about us and the state of our knowledge when we consider such statements, not about the statements themselves or their truth or their necessity. It does not mean that necessary truths do not state anything, or anything about the world.

I think the claim that necessary truths are "empty" or "devoid of factual content" is best seen as an attempt to express a negative metaphysical verdict about the necessity of necessary truths: that there is no such necessity in the world as it is independently of us. That verdict would be supported by showing that the contents of our concepts and the relations among them are in some way simply 'our' contribution to the conception of the world we have developed—something 'we' alone are responsible for or freely decide on, and nothing in the way things are independently of us. If that could be shown to hold of all necessary truths, and if it could then be shown that all such truths are 'true solely in virtue of' what is included in our concepts and the relations among them, as the doctrine of analyticity implies, then necessary truths would have been shown to be products of nothing more than our own efforts to understand the world in the ways we do. What we ourselves bring to that task would be enough to account for both the necessity of the necessary truths we accept and our a priori knowledge of them.

That was the appeal of the full, rich notion of the analyticity of necessary truth. But how is it to be shown that the contents of our concepts are something that 'we' are responsible for or that is 'up to us'? And how is it to be shown that the necessary truths we accept are nothing more than by-products of whatever creative sovereignty we enjoy with

---

13. Ibid., p. 80.

respect to the contents of our concepts and what they imply? This is the first question to be asked about a negative metaphysical verdict: how is it to be reached?

Human freedom or agency in the formation and employment of concepts is thought to be indicated by the presence or availability of alternatives. We think of the world in terms of certain concepts and ways of thinking, but it seems that things could have been different in that respect. We could have thought in different ways, with different concepts. On the assumption that the contents of our concepts are the source of the necessary truths we accept, it might seem that with different concepts we would accept quite different necessary truths—those expressing the contents of those different concepts. Can it be shown that the necessity of the necessary truths we now accept is therefore due to our having adopted the concepts or ways of thinking we now actually employ? Something like this appears to be required for full metaphysical success in the unmasking appeal to the analyticity of necessary truth. It is perhaps enough to express the requirement in this stark form to be struck by the difficulty of ever fulfilling it.

The difficulty can be seen perhaps most clearly by considering first the case of language. It was once widely held that necessary truth finds its source only in language; that all necessary truths are analytic in the sense of being true solely in virtue of the meanings of the words in which they are expressed. One obvious attraction of the appeal to language is that what the words we use mean is something that is in the relevantly broad sense 'up to us.' What words mean depends on what speakers do, and speakers could have behaved differently from the ways they behave now. If speakers had spoken differently in the past, or if we now made certain decisions about our words that are at least theoretically open to us, the sounds and marks we now use to say what we say would mean something different from what they mean now. And it looks as if the way things are in the independent world would not have to be otherwise different in order for that to be so.

Although how we speak and what our words mean are up to us in those ways, that does nothing to show that the truth of what we say depends on our acting with our words as we now do. The most it shows is that the means we use to express the truths we now accept is in a broad sense up to us, but not the truth or the necessity of anything we now accept. That the English word 'and' is used to express conjunction is something that could have been otherwise. If that word had not been used to form a compound predicate that is true of something if and only if both the conjoined predicates are true of it, the sentence 'Everything that is red and round is round,' whatever it would then have meant, would not have expressed the necessary truth it now expresses. But that does not show that the necessity with which everything that is red and round is round is due to our using the word 'and' in the ways we now do.

There is a very general reason for this. It applies to any appeal to linguistic practice or the conventional use of words as well as to explicit definitions or specifications of meaning. A word or expression that is said to have a certain meaning or is assigned a meaning by stipulation is mentioned, not used, in that description or stipulation. The meaning given to a word can be anything we please; in that respect there is complete freedom. But the words used in stating what the meaning of that mentioned expression is or is to be must themselves be used with already determinate meanings in specifying what the new word is to mean. Only if that is so will the specification succeed in stating some definite conditions that the introduced expression must fulfill to have the meaning assigned to it.

This means that what is implied by fulfillment of the conditions stated in the specification of an expression's meaning is not itself affected by the assigning of those conditions of application to the expression then being introduced. Whether a description of an expression's current meaning is correct depends on whether it is true that the expression correctly applies to something if and only if the conditions stated in that description are fulfilled. A stipulation or assignment of meaning to an expression that does not already have a meaning does not have to answer to any prior conditions. But the only elements of freedom in such a stipulation are the choice of the expression and the choice of the conditions that are to give it its meaning.

If the word 'bachelor' is explicitly defined or stipulated to be true of all and only unmarried adult males, the sentence 'All bachelors are unmarried' will then express something that is necessarily true. But the necessary truth of what is then expressed by those words does not depend on that stipulation's having been made. It is necessarily true, prior to and independently of that action of assigning that meaning to the word 'bachelor,' that all unmarried adult males are unmarried. That is why the new sentence with the new word 'bachelors' in the place of 'unmarried adult males' expresses a necessary truth. But the necessity of that truth is not thereby shown to be the result of any act of stipulation or definition. It has not been shown to find its source in, or hold 'in virtue of,' anything 'we' do in assigning that meaning to that word.

The point holds even when a whole language or linguistic framework is to be set up and given meaning. Rules for the combination of symbols into well-formed expressions of a language can be laid down by explicit convention or stipulation, along with further rules for deriving one well-formed expression from another to form legitimate sequences of such expressions. Semantical rules can be added, specifying the reference of some of the expressions and the conditions under which some expressions will say something true. All this will make it possible to pick out in purely linguistic terms some expressions of that constructed language that say something that is necessarily true.

This might make it look as if the necessary truths expressed by those newly constructed sentences are themselves by-products of this stipulative language-fixing alone. But that is not so. A demonstration that certain sentences of the new language say something that is necessarily true must be carried out in a meta-language using expressions with already-determinate meanings to say something about the so-far merely mentioned expressions of the constructed language. The necessities that those demonstrations depend on and exploit are therefore prior to and independent of the specification and adoption of the rules of the new language. What is more, for any interesting set of logical and mathematical truths that can be circumscribed by such linguistic means, the logical and mathematical resources of the meta-language used to pick them out must be richer than the domain of logical and mathematical truths thereby picked out by the stipulated rules of the constructed language. It is not possible to show all logical and mathematical truths to be consequences of rules laid down for the use or meaning of certain expressions. Some necessities remain independent of whatever is determinately fixed by specifying rules of a particular linguistic framework. Such was the fate of the promising-sounding idea that logical and mathematical truths are all true by virtue of the meanings of words or the rules of a linguistic framework.

What bedevils all attempts to create meanings of expressions by stipulation alone in an attempt to generate necessary truths by fiat or convention is that the stipulation must use some expressions with already-determinate meanings. Recognizing the difficulty can perhaps encourage the hope of declaring certain things true by fiat or convention more directly, without assigning meanings to particular linguistic expressions at all. It is not at all clear how something could be or be made or become true simply by being declared true. But even if we could simply declare something to be true, we could not account for the truth or the necessity of all the necessary truths we accept as deriving from some such fiat or declaration.

We could not declare each necessary truth to be true one by one; that would be a task without end. Any declaration or convention that could achieve the desired end would therefore have to be general in form, declaring as true all statements of a certain kind. But then to conclude from that general declaration that a particular statement of that kind is true would require the truth of a conditional statement linking the two. That conditional would not yet have been declared true. To declare that conditional statement true in turn would lead only to acceptance of the truth of the particular statement in question. To reach the truth of any other particular statement from that same general declaration of truth would require that yet another conditional statement be explicitly declared to be true, and so on without end.[14] This means that not all the necessities relied on in moving from declarations of truth to the truth of all the necessary truths we accept could themselves be generated by nothing more than such declarations.

This is a difficulty for any *linguistic* theory according to which necessary truths are true solely in virtue of the meanings of the words in which they are expressed. What seemed to count in favor of this kind of theory of necessary truth was the presence of alternatives: the possibility of using different words with different meanings or making different decisions or declarations about what words are to mean. But what lies behind the appeal to analyticity as an explanation of necessary truth is deeper than a concern with words or the linguistic expression of thoughts. It involves a view of thought itself. It sees our conception of the world as a combination of two distinct factors, each with its own separate source. We must have some concepts or ways of thinking in order to think or believe anything at all, but what concepts we have, and what they contain, is said to be up to us, and is our contribution alone. In this we exercise our conceptual sovereignty.

Whether what we formulate and believe about the contingent world in terms of the concepts we use is true or not depends on how things are independently of us. The truth or falsity of those beliefs in contingent fact must answer to the way things are. But the idea is that that is not true of the necessary truths expressing the contents of the concepts we use even in those contingent beliefs. Those truths and that necessity are said to be our own contribution, and to hold independently of all the ways things happen to be.

What is thought to show that our concepts are our contribution alone is that there are alternatives to the concepts we have, and we are in a certain sense free to choose among them. If that were not so, and our concepts were the only concepts we could have, we could not understand

---

14. See W. V. Quine, "Truth by Convention," in his *The Ways of Paradox*, Random House, New York, 1966, drawing on the classic Lewis Carroll, "What the Tortoise Said to Achilles," *Mind* 1895.

those concepts to represent only our own contribution to our understanding of the world. What we recognized to be necessarily true in virtue of the contents of those concepts would present itself to us as part of the way things simply must be.[15] That would leave our a priori knowledge of those truths unexplained. It is essential to the appeal to analyticity as an explanation of our a priori knowledge of necessary truth that we are said to enjoy a certain 'freedom' in choosing which concepts to use in making sense of what the world presents us with.

We are said to be free in that the adoption or possession of a concept is not forced on us by anything that happens in the independent world. We *can* hold on to a set of concepts and their associated necessary truths whatever the world might present us with. Or we *can* abandon them if we find that that way of thinking no longer best serves our intellectual purposes. Neither decision is forced or implied by anything in the independent world. We decide on "pragmatic" grounds, on the basis of which way of thinking, all things considered, will be most helpful in understanding the world. This independence from experience is essential to the knowledge in question being a priori. Adoption of a new set of concepts carries with it acceptance of a new set of analytic and therefore necessary truths that were not in the picture before. Of course those new concepts might eventually prove inadequate in their turn. That again will be determined by the degree of our overall success in understanding the world in terms of them, not because their inadequacy is implied by any experience we might have of the world.

It is crucial to the success of this view that when concepts are abandoned in favor of others that better serve our purposes, the necessary truths expressing the contents of those concepts that were accepted in the past are not rejected because they have been shown by experience to be false. That would mean that their acceptance or rejection was based on experience, and so would be a posteriori. And that is inconsistent with the fundamental epistemological assumption on which this whole view rests: that all knowledge of necessary truths is a priori. To preserve that assumption in the face of conceptual change it must be maintained that to abandon a set of concepts and the necessary truths that express their contents is not to reject those necessary truths as false. It is simply to abandon one set of potential intellectual instruments in favor of another that looks as if it will do a better job. There is no implication of

---

15. This fundamental point was stressed and developed to most illuminating effect by C. I. Lewis, *Mind and the World Order*, Dover, New York, 1956 (originally published 1929), esp. ch. 7.

falsity in such a change because, as C. I. Lewis put it, "the alternative to a definition or rule is not its falsity but merely its abandonment in favor of some other."[16] When such a change occurs,

> *the truth remains unaltered and new truth and old truth do not contradict.* Categories and concepts do not literally change; they are simply given up and replaced by new ones.[17]

This way of understanding conceptual change is essential to defending the a priori character of the knowledge of necessary truths which (according to the doctrine of analyticity) express nothing more than the contents of concepts. The choice of concepts and their corresponding truths must be independent of anything forced or implied by actual or possible experience. But this view faces a real difficulty. The free choice in question is a choice only of the adoption or possession of certain concepts rather than others. When a set of concepts is abandoned by such a decision the necessity and the truth of the statements expressing the contents of those abandoned concepts are not affected. Since 'old' necessary truth and 'new' necessary truth do not conflict, freedom of conceptual choice does not show that those necessities themselves hold only as a result of our having made the choices we have made. The 'old' necessary truths remain necessarily true whatever we have decided. So the 'new' necessary truths are not shown to be true or to be necessary as a result of our decision to adopt some new concepts either.

Someone who believed that concepts or properties stand in fixed necessary relations to one another, and that the truths expressing those relations hold necessarily quite independently of any decisions by us, could still agree that it is 'up to us' to decide which concepts to choose in trying to understand the world. We might abandon some intellectual instruments theoretically available to us in favor of others that we think will help make better sense of the way things are. Although the choice would be up to us, on this view neither the truth nor the necessity of the analytic truths that express the contents of the concepts we choose would be up to us. Their truth and their necessity would not depend in any way on our strategic decisions about which concepts to use. This shows in another way what we saw earlier: that 'mere' analyticity— necessary truths' being true solely in virtue of the contents of their constituent concepts—is not alone sufficient to show that necessary truths are 'empty' or 'devoid of factual content.' It is not enough to support a

---

16. Ibid., p. 232.
17. Ibid., p. 268 (italics in text).

negative metaphysical verdict about necessity as part of the independent world.[18]

Reaching that verdict requires that the doctrine of analyticity be accompanied by the further idea of the 'emptiness' or lack of 'factual content' of necessary truths. The necessity is then to be seen as due only to 'us' or to something we are 'responsible' for, and not to the way things are independently of us. That was meant to be shown by the availability of alternatives to our present concepts and our freedom to choose among them independently of the dictates of experience. But the conceptual choices 'we' are responsible for reach only as far as the selection of this or that concept for our intellectual purposes. It is a choice or decision about which concepts we should accept and make use of. But choosing as we do has no effect on the truth or falsity of what we thereby come to accept. Even if all necessary truths are analytic in the sense of expressing nothing more than the contents of concepts, our making such a conceptual decision does not show that the necessary truths we then accept are simply products of that choice or decision.

This is not to deny that our *acceptance* or *employment* of those truths is a result of something we do and are responsible for. But that is true of our acceptance of everything we accept, including what we take to be contingent truths about the way things happen to be. We accept and employ what we accept about the world in the interest of making the best sense of everything the world presents us with. That is something we are responsible for. But that does not imply that the truth of any of the things we accept is explained or somehow generated by our doing what we do. So it does not show that some of the things we accept say nothing about what is so in the world independently of us.

Any attempt to explain the 'ground' or 'source' of the necessity of necessary truths by appealing to something we do or something we are responsible for—whether it be the meanings we assign to words or linguistic frameworks or languages or the adoption of concepts or 'conceptual schemes'—faces what appears to be an insurmountable general obstacle. The problem lies in the very idea of explaining or accounting for an 'absolute' necessity.

To understand the necessity of necessary truths as depending on something that in some way accounts for it or is responsible for it we would have to recognize that if it had not been for that explanatory factor, whatever it might be, the truths in question would not have been necessary or

---

18. See pp. 64–66 above.

perhaps even true. That seems to be required for any explanation of something as due to something else. But then to accept such an explanation of necessity we would have to acknowledge that if it had not been for that explanatory factor the necessary truth in question would not have been necessary or perhaps even true. That means we would have to grant at least the possibility of circumstances in which something that we regard as necessarily true would not have been true or would not have been necessarily true. But no one could consistently grant such a thing. To concede that there are possible circumstances in which something one holds to be necessarily true would not have been true or would not have held necessarily would be to concede that it is not necessarily true after all—that there are possible circumstances in which it would not be true or necessarily true. The very idea of something's being absolutely necessary seems to preclude 'explaining' its 'source' along any such lines.

This represents an obstacle to understanding something's being necessarily true as generated by or arising from something contingent that would explain it. And we have seen how the attempt to explain even our *acceptance* of certain things as necessarily true presupposes our acceptance of other necessities whose acceptance therefore is not explained in that same way. All this suggests the indispensability of the idea of necessity and the impossibility of explaining it or defining it in different but equivalent terms. It certainly is difficult to see how anyone could think at all, or could move through a series of thoughts from one thing to another, without recognizing that certain things hold, or fail to hold, necessarily. But if the necessity of certain things must be accepted by anyone who can think anything, then some necessities would have to be accepted even in an attempt to show that nothing really holds with necessity in the independent world. A negative metaphysical verdict about necessity could therefore not be consistently arrived at by any such unmasking route. The 'conclusion' could not be accepted consistently with accepting everything that is needed in order to reach it.

In the case of causal or subjunctive conditional modality, the threat of this kind of inconsistency encouraged acceptance of some form or other of reductionism. The hope was that the very contents of what would otherwise be metaphysically suspicious modal beliefs would thereby be shown to be equivalent to something familiar and unproblematically non-modal. That was the promise of a 'regularity' analysis of the idea of causation, whether the regularities were taken to hold only among observed objects of certain kinds or also among happenings in our minds when we observe such objects. This turned out to be an unpromising strategy in the case of causation. Either there remained an unreduced modal element in the analysis, or *every* correlation between things turned out to be causal, or causal connections hold only between things that human beings have actually observed.

The prospects of a reduction of the idea of 'absolute' necessity along similar lines are no better, to say the least. There is simply no hope of reducing the contents of the idea of absolute necessity to anything about us and our ways of thinking of and responding to the world. All facts of human beings' taking or being disposed to take certain distinctive attitudes to some of the things they believe are contingent and could have been otherwise. But no combination of such facts, as long as it remained contingent, could be equivalent to something's being necessarily true. No form of reduction or explanation with any hope of success can therefore seek an equivalence between contingent facts of our having certain responses or attitudes and something's holding necessarily.

The idea we have of something's being necessarily true is the idea of its holding with no possibility of its being or having been otherwise. That same idea is present in the thought of one thing's being a consequence of another in the sense that it *must* be true, with no possibility of its being false, *if* the other thing is true. This is often described as 'logical necessity,' with 'logical' truth and 'logical' consequence defined in purely 'logical' terms. This might appear to offer an acceptable explanation or perhaps even a replacement of the allegedly problematic modal ideas of necessity and possibility.

Calling the necessity of a truth or the necessity of a consequence 'logical' can appear to indicate the 'source' or 'ground' of that necessity as lying somehow in logic. That would require a determinate limit to what is included within logic and what is not, with some account of how we can tell where the limit lies. But even with some fixed demarcation of logic it would raise the puzzle of how anything to be found in logic (or anywhere else, for that matter) could be understood to be the 'source' or 'ground' or explanation of the necessity of something that is necessarily so. We have seen reason to doubt the possibility or even the intelligibility of something's *explaining* or accounting for necessity in general in a way that does not presuppose it.

Of course, speaking of 'logical' truth or consequence would represent no advance in understanding if it meant only that the truth in question could not *possibly* have been false, or that if one proposition is a 'logical' consequence of another it is not *possible* (or logically possible) for the one to be false if the other is true. It would be no better explanation to invoke the idea of something's being true, or not true 'in every possible world.'

A more austere conception of 'logical' truth or 'logical' consequence says that a sentence expresses a logical truth in a particular language if every result of assigning objects of the appropriate kinds to all of the non-logical terms of that sentence is itself true; if every such 'interpretation' of the sentence-frame yields a truth. This requires a specification in advance of which terms in a given vocabulary count as logical and which do not. Taking some such category of terms as fixed, perhaps by arbitrarily listing all the terms that are to count as logical, a successful specification of the rules of the language would serve to distinguish all those sentences in the given vocabulary that express 'logical' truths in the sense of this definition from those that do not. The truths would be 'logical' in the sense that their truth-value remains the same under all variations in the interpretation of all their non-logical constituent terms.

There are many alternative ways of specifying a language and fixing a set of logical terms that would define 'logical' truth and consequence in non-equivalent ways, even given the same set of logical terms. And there are complexities to be attended to in formulating particular definitions that capture all and only the consequences we think do or should hold. But for our general purposes here we can put those details to one side and focus on the relation between 'logical' truth or consequence defined in this way and our ideas of necessity and possibility.

For one thing, it is clear that there is no possibility of specifying a vocabulary and a set of logical terms and the rules of a language that could serve in this way to pick out all and only all the truths that hold necessarily. This is the fundamental point noted earlier.[19] A particular specification of a class of 'logical' truths might contain only truths that hold necessarily, but that would determine only the extension of that class. The specification would serve to pick out a class of truths solely by means of their 'logical' form, but it would not show that the idea of 'logical' form or the resulting definition of 'logical' truth contains or expresses, let alone replaces or explains, the idea of necessity. With appropriate specification of logical terms, the logical form exhibited by the sentence 'Everything that is red and round is round' enables us to see that it expresses something that is necessarily true, just as from the logical form exhibited by the sentences 'a is red and round' and 'a is round' we can see that if the first is true the second must be true. But those modal facts are not expressed in what the definition of 'logical' truth or consequence says is true of those sentences.

A definition of 'logical' truth along these lines says that on *every* interpretation of all the non-logical components of a sentence, each

---

19. See p. 72 above.

particular instance of its sentence-frame comes out true. There is nothing distinctively modal in that universal generalization. Nor is there anything distinctively modal in saying of a conditional sentence that *no* interpretation of all its non-logical components yields an instance with a true antecedent and a false consequent. That is what this definition says it means to say that the consequent of a conditional sentence is a 'logical' consequence of its antecedent, and hence that the conditional is a 'logical' truth. But that is not all we mean when we say that the consequent of a certain conditional statement *must* be true if the antecedent is true, or that the whole conditional sentence is necessarily true and could not possibly have been false.[20]

Of course, if one statement is a 'logical' consequence of another according to this definition, and the first statement is true, then the second must be true. But that is not what we mean in saying simply that the one statement is a consequence of the other. We mean that if the first is true the second must be true. It might be true of a certain book that on every page on which the first sentence is true the second sentence on that page is also true. Given that universal generalization, and the fact that the first sentence on page 18 of that book is true, the second sentence on page 18 must also be true. But that does not mean that the second sentence on page 18 is a consequence of the first sentence on that page. We cannot say simply and without qualification that the second sentence must be true if the first sentence is true. That is what we mean in speaking of the relation of consequence between two sentences; it is not possible for the first to be true and the second false. A definition of 'logical' truth or 'logical' consequence expressed only in a universal generalization about *all* interpretations of all non-logical terms of the sentence makes no appeal to the modal idea of possibility, and so says nothing about all *possible* interpretations.

This is not to say that there is anything unsatisfactory or even suspicious about the idea of 'logical' truth or 'logical' consequence so defined. On the contrary. It is a precisely definable mathematical notion applied in the meta-theory of logic and mathematics to pick out actual classes of truths in a specified vocabulary.[21] It can accordingly be used to pick out particular classes of truths of many different kinds. But when it picks

---

20. J. Etchemendy gives a very clear and illuminating treatment of issues concerning the modality of logical consequence in his *The Concept of Logical Consequence*, Harvard University Press, Cambridge, Mass., 1990.

21. A truth's being 'logical' in this sense does not imply anything about the epistemic status of that truth, as Quine has stressed (see e.g., "Carnap and Logical Truth," in *Ways of Paradox*). The same holds for its modal status.

out in this way a set of truths all of which hold necessarily, it does not itself contain or express that modal idea of necessity. It could be said that this is no defect in the idea of 'logical' truth or consequence, since mathematics itself does not really need that idea of necessity. For any actual mathematical theory, truth and proof might be said to be enough, with the validity of proofs in the theory defined by this definition of logical consequence. But we all have and use the idea of necessity in recognizing that many things we believe and know, including propositions of logic and mathematics, must be true, or that certain things *must* be so if certain other things are so. We have and use the idea that such things differ in their modality from things we recognize could have been otherwise. And we need the modal idea of necessity in acknowledging the epistemic guarantee provided by proof: that *if* the premises are true the conclusion *must* be true. To omit the modal element from our idea of consequence would leave us with less than we have and need to express the necessities we believe in.

One role the idea of necessity can be seen to play in our thought is that in recognizing that the truth of one proposition implies the truth of another we can thereby *know* the second to be true if we know the first is true. But that does not mean that necessity is something "epistemic," or that it can be explained by its playing that role in our coming to know things on the basis of something else. The necessity that enables us to know that one proposition must be true if a certain other proposition is true is something we see to hold between the truth of the two propositions. It is not a feature of us or of the state of our knowledge. Nor is the necessity some "compulsion" we might feel or some "demand" we think we are under to accept the second proposition, given that we accept the first. Whatever pressure or compulsion we might feel to accept the proposition in the face of the necessity comes from our recognition of the necessity of the connection between the truth of the two propositions; if the first is true the second must be true. What we thereby recognize is nothing about human knowledge or how to get it or how to extend it.

The unavailability of any illuminating reduction of the idea of necessity can still leave us with the question of what exactly is said when we declare something to be not just true and not just logically true but necessarily true. What is added, and what point do we make in adding it? What do these modal ideas do for us that we could not do without them? These are questions about the meaning and distinctive role of modal ideas in our thought about the world. That is a rich and complex subject, avidly pursued by many philosophers, sometimes even without deeper metaphysical aspirations. But if the idea of necessity is truly irreducible to non-modal terms, as it seems to be, it will not be possible to say much that is helpful to those who find the whole idea of necessity and possibility metaphysically problematic. Whatever is said will seem to help itself to some of the very modal ideas whose use is meant to be accounted for.

It obviously would not advance understanding of our use of the idea of necessity to say (however truly) that one thing we can do with that idea that we could not do without it is to say of some truths that they hold necessarily and of others that they do not. It might look as if a more satisfying kind of explanation of our practice could be given by concentrating instead on the reasons and attitudes that lead us to ascribe necessity to some but not all of the truths we accept. This would be to concede that the idea of necessity is irreducible, and to look instead at the grounds on which we typically apply the term, or the point or significance of applying it as we do, rather than at any set of conditions regarded as equivalent to its meaning.

This might seem to keep alive the prospect of accepting a negative metaphysical verdict about 'absolute' necessity along the lines that once seemed promising for causal or counterfactual conditional necessity. Understanding the conditions under which we apply the problematic terms might be expected to reveal that the necessity we appear to speak of in such judgments is not to be found in the world independent of us; that it "has its locus elsewhere,"[22] in Ernest Nagel's phrase. Necessity is to be understood somehow in terms of something true of us, in our taking the attitudes we do, and not straightforwardly as part of the independent world we believe in.

I think difficulties exactly parallel to those we found in trying to apply this strategy to the idea of causation arise in this case as well. For one thing, as we saw in that case, even an accurate description of the conditions under which we do and do not ascribe necessity to something is not enough to explain *what* we so ascribe to a truth when we regard it as holding necessarily. Asserting or believing that something holds necessarily are only two of the many different attitudes we can take toward the necessity of something. We can ask or wonder whether something or other is necessarily true, or imagine or hypothesize that it is, without knowing whether it is necessarily true or not, and so without being in a position to assert or believe that it is. When we ask or wonder whether a certain proposition holds necessarily we do not ask or wonder

---

22. Ernest Nagel, *The Structure of Science*, Harcourt, Brace, and World, New York, 1961, p. 56 (see p. 40 above).

whether the conditions for our asserting that it holds necessarily are fulfilled; if we are still asking or wondering, we usually know they are not. We ask or wonder whether the proposition holds necessarily; whether what would be said in asserting that it holds necessarily is true. A description of the conditions under which we would assert it does not necessarily tell us what we would assert if we did assert it under those conditions.

Furthermore, if the prospect of reaching a negative metaphysical verdict about necessity is to remain open, the role of the idea of necessity and our reasons for applying it as we do must be described without making essential use of that very idea or presupposing an unexplained understanding of it on our part. It looks as if any description of our practice that met these strict constraints could do little to explain the distinctive use we make of the term 'necessary' and its modal companions.

Even if we found some conditions describable in fully non-modal terms that are in fact fulfilled when and only when we ascribe necessity to something we believe, which seems to me unlikely, it would indicate only when we do and do not ascribe necessity to something, not what we are doing or saying in ascribing it. A fuller description of our use of the term 'necessary' would seek to identify our reasons for ascribing it as we do. But to keep alive the prospect of reaching a negative metaphysical verdict we can consistently accept, those reasons we recognize must be described without making essential use of the problematic modal terms.

For instance, we recognize the impossibility of the falsity of a proposition as reason to believe that it holds necessarily. But that description of our practice ascribes to us a still-unexplained modal attitude, and so makes no advance in explaining the modal vocabulary or our use of it. But if what we take to be reason to ascribe necessity to something is described only in non-modal terms, it would leave unexplained how we can see such a non-modal state of affairs as reason to ascribe the distinct modal status of necessity to something. With only a non-modal description of the conditions, our practice of ascribing necessity for such a reason would not make sense. It is not only a question of explaining our taking such-and-such as reason to ascribe necessity. A description of our practice must give some account not only of the reasons but also of what we think they give us reason to do: to ascribe necessity to something. If that is part of what must be understood to make the right kind of sense of what we do, how could we do it without some understanding of the idea of necessity?

One possibility of advance has been thought to lie in the fact that the propositions to which we ascribe necessary truth are all such that we cannot clearly conceive of what it would be like for them to be false. If that is indeed a fact about us, it might seem to promise some understanding of our practice with terms like 'necessary' without making use of those modal terms themselves or presupposing any unexplained use of them on our part. The idea is not that we regard it as 'absolutely' impossible for us to conceive or make anything of the thought of the falsity of the propositions in question. It is just that, as a matter of fact, however hard we try, nothing we do manages to bring about a clear conception of what the falsity of those propositions would amount to.

I think it must be admitted that we cannot clearly conceive of the falsity of propositions we correctly believe to hold necessarily. Whether it is also true of propositions about which we ask or wonder whether they hold necessarily or not, I am not so sure. It is probably not a good idea to put very much weight on what we can or cannot clearly conceive, as if it is something that could be reliably determined independently of everything else we know or think we know about the world. But even granting that we are unable to conceive of the falsity of those propositions we regard as necessary, that inability of ours is not what we mention or attribute to those propositions when we say that they are necessarily true. What we ascribe to them is necessary truth, or the impossibility of their falsity, not anything about ourselves or our inability to conceive of something.

If our inability to clearly conceive of the falsity of certain propositions is to play a part in helping explain the use we make of modal terms like 'necessary,' that inability cannot be seen as simply a limitation we happen to operate under. If we regard it as a limitation we are subject to as things are now, but which we might have been free of if things had been different in certain ways, we could no longer hold those propositions to be necessarily true. To imagine that greater powers of conception could have enabled us to conceive of their falsity would be to concede that their falsity is a conceivable possibility and so their truth, if they have it, does not hold necessarily.

The fact that when we ascribe necessity to a certain proposition we do not assert that we are unable to conceive of its falsity, and the fact that its necessity cannot be validly inferred from our inability to conceive of its falsity, shows that inconceivability of falsity, in so far as we can recognize it, is no test or criterion of necessary truth. That will be granted by many who nonetheless look to the limitations of our powers of conception as the key to a proper understanding of our modal practices.

Our inability to conceive of the falsity of certain propositions is something Simon Blackburn, for instance, thinks a "projectivist" theorist can make "good use" of.[23]

He thinks our acknowledged inability to conceive of the falsity of certain propositions is what is "projected" onto or expressed in the thought that those things could not be true—"that their negations are necessary."[24] In ascribing necessity to something in this way we come to accept a world that is thereby seen to be modally 'richer' than we could think of it as being without that new idea.

As in his account of our 'projection' of the modal idea of causal dependence out of the non-causal facts he thinks we originally observe, Blackburn does not explain here how we come to "project" our recognized inability into an ascription of necessity to something. He appears to acknowledge a certain "movement" of thought in the sense that we do find ourselves unable to conceive of the falsity of certain propositions, and we do ascribe necessity to those propositions. There does seem to be a difference between those two attitudes; thinking the one thing is not the same as thinking the other. But Blackburn holds that we make "no step" from the one to the other. He draws on a parallel he sees with moral judgment as "projected" from "sentiment" to explain what he has in mind. In moral judgment, he says,

> when the sentiments are strong and nothing on the cards explains them by the presence of defects, we go ahead and moralize. . . . The 'step' from a fully integrated sentiment of sufficient strength to the moral expression now becomes no step at all: the moral is just the vocabulary in which to express that state.[25]

Of course we make no "step" from sentiment to "moralizing" if we already have the moral vocabulary at hand and are proficient in its use. "We go ahead and moralize"; we employ the moral vocabulary we already understand and use. But some account is still needed of the relation between our feeling a certain "sentiment" on the one hand and our competence in and distinctive understanding of the moral vocabulary on the other. Even if there is no "step" from the one to the other for the fully competent moral thinker, the two are not the same. Further explanation is needed, unless having what Blackburn calls a "fully integrated sentiment of sufficient strength" is already to have a moral attitude. There would then be no difference between the two, but the 'sentiment' would not help explain the moral attitude.

23. S. Blackburn, "Morals and Modals," in his *Essays in Quasi-Realism*, Oxford University Press, Oxford, 1993, p. 70.

24. Ibid.

25. Ibid.

The presumed parallel in the case of necessity is that, in Blackburn's words, having "arrived at the residual class of propositions of whose truth we can make nothing . . . we express ourselves by saying that they cannot be true—that their negations are necessary."[26] But this too gives no account of how, starting from our inability to make anything of the truth of certain propositions, we come to understand and use the idea of necessity we employ in saying "their negations are necessary." We do say and believe such modally expressed things, but what we then say differs from what we say and believe about our inability to conceive of the falsity of the propositions. A strict parallel to what Blackburn says about moral judgment would be to say "The 'step' from acknowledging the class of propositions of whose truth we can make nothing to the modal expression now becomes no step at all: the modal is just the vocabulary we use to express that acknowledgement." But that is not so; the two 'vocabularies' and the kinds of things we say with them are different. Even if in calling something necessarily true we 'acknowledge' that we can make nothing of its falsity, that is not what we say of it when we say it holds necessarily. Blackburn concedes that there is a special difficulty in the case of necessity in particular. Unlike the explanation of our thoughts about causation and morality, with necessity "we cannot explain *naturalistically* our own failure to see what it would be for [the negations of the propositions we regard as necessary] to be true."[27] He takes this to reveal something residually "surd" in our understanding of necessity; the "modalist," he thinks, cannot be "completely aware of the genesis and justification of his activity" as Blackburn thinks the "moralist" (and presumably the causal 'projectivist') can. It remains to be seen whether the "moralist" is in a more favorable position here.[28]

The obstacle Blackburn recognizes for the "modalist" is that he cannot regard our inability to conceive of the opposite of something as a contingent limitation that might have been otherwise. That would undermine our commitment to the necessity of those propositions whose falsity we cannot conceive of. That seems right, as we saw earlier.[29] To allow that we would have been able to conceive of the falsity of certain propositions if things had been different in certain ways is to allow that under those circumstances those propositions could have been false. But then they are not necessarily true. So no 'naturalistic'

---

26. Ibid
27. Ibid.
28. I take up this question in chapter 4 below.
29. See pp. 76–77 above.

explanation of our inability that appeals to incapacities we have but might have lacked is acceptable.

That does not mean there can be no explanation at all of our inability to conceive of the falsity of those propositions we regard as necessary. That could be explained by the fact that if a proposition holds necessarily it is impossible for there to be any circumstances in which it is false. There would then be no such possibility for us to conceive of; no wonder we cannot conceive of it. But that is not what Blackburn calls a 'naturalistic' explanation. It is disqualified for his purposes because it makes essential use of the otherwise unexplained modal notions of necessity and impossibility.

A 'naturalistic' explanation of the kind Blackburn insists on appeals only to what is so in a metaphysically 'purified' world that contains no unexplained necessities or possibilities. That is how it appears to leave open the prospect of arriving at a negative metaphysical verdict about necessity. That is also what makes for something essentially "surd" in the understanding Blackburn offers of our modal thoughts. No 'naturalistic' explanation of them can be given. But if no adequate description of the thoughts of those whose modal ideas are to be accounted for can be given without making essential use of those modal notions themselves, so much the worse for the prospects of reaching a negative metaphysical verdict about necessity by that route.

In ascribing necessity to a truth we take a step beyond whatever thoughts and attitudes not involving that modality were involved in our coming to ascribe it. We make a stronger claim, with a distinct modality. A different and additional attitude is involved, and any adequate description of our practice must describe and account for that difference. We who possess and understand the modal ideas needed to express that additional attitude can understand and describe that difference. If the modal notions we employ are irreducible to others that do not presuppose them, it cannot be captured in non-modal terms alone.

In this respect there is a parallel with our idea of truth. In trying to determine what is so, we assess the considerations in favor of accepting a certain proposition and then declare it to be true (or false). In drawing that conclusion, we do not simply assert something about the strength of the considerations that lead us to draw it or the extent to which we find them persuasive. In asserting the proposition as true we take a new step and say something different and stronger than anything about our attitudes or the support for asserting what we do. The content of what we assert, or the idea of truth we possess in making the assertion, cannot be explained solely in terms of our having the grounds or bases on which we assert it.

No description of our practice of assertion that restricted itself to the considerations that lead to our making assertions, or to the strength of the grounds that influence us, could adequately capture the distinctive character and significance of assertion or the idea of truth that is embodied and expressed in it. In asserting or accepting something as true we show our understanding of an idea of truth whose meaning is not exhausted in any such conditions alone. The distinctiveness and irreducibility of the idea of necessity represents a similar challenge to those who would look only to the grounds or bases of our holding the modal attitudes we do to explain those modal ideas themselves and the significance of our applying them as we do.

There still remains the feeling that no satisfactory explanation of necessity or of what we are doing in ascribing it as we do has really been given. Certainly nothing has been done that provides the kind of metaphysical understanding of necessity we have been pursuing. Nothing has been said "from outside" the allegedly problematic domain of modal terms to explain in alternative terms what really goes on "inside" it. It must be granted that nothing along those lines has been said or explained. That is perhaps not surprising, given the irreducibility of the modal domain. Irreducibility can make it seem that nothing could possibly satisfy those who feel that necessity has still not really been explained. But what kind of satisfaction do we seek? And what exactly is the nature and source of the disappointment we can feel in not having it?

One dissatisfaction in the face of the irreducibility of the idea of necessity is the feeling that it leaves it a mystery how we ever come to understand and apply modal notions in the first place. We know it is not impossible, since we do possess and understand the modal vocabulary. And we know we do not acquire it by recognizing conditions expressible in non-modal terms that we find to be sufficient for the correct application of those richer modal ideas. The same is true of our understanding of the irreducible modal idea of causal or counterfactual dependence. Experience of nothing more than correlations between similar phenomena is not sufficient for their application.

If the mystery is how anyone could get either of these modal ideas in the first place, it is worth remembering that each of us gets those ideas, as we get all our ideas, by becoming socialized into a language and culture that already has them. We gain capacities we could never acquire on our own, if we were restricted only to bombardments by the surrounding world with no way to think further about what is happening to us. But acknowledging the undeniable effects of socialization can still leave us dissatisfied. At best it seems to explain only how some people get certain ideas from others who already have them. But it does not explain in general what those ideas are, how anyone at all ever comes to have them, or what we are all doing in applying them as we do.

I think all this must be granted, however we might feel about it. There is no way of constructing the contents of those distinctively modal ideas out of whatever non-modal materials might be thought to be available to us. Nor does any known variety of a 'projectivist' theory succeed in identifying some maneuver by which we can be seen to move in thought from such non-modal beginnings to the richness of the modal vocabularies we know we now possess. But there is no question that that is where we have all ended up. We do have those ideas, and by making use of them as we do we can describe their significance and what they make it possible for us to do that we could not do without them.

This is not to deny that there are deep and puzzling aspects of the modal vocabulary that are still not well understood. We can profit from further careful study of those notions quite apart from any metaphysical anxieties about their status in reality. But in the face of that metaphysical question, the fact that we can investigate those ideas and appreciate their complexity and pervasiveness only "from within" an understanding and acceptance of them can feel like a disappointing limitation. There is probably no way of overcoming that disappointment completely, if it is strongly felt. Maybe the most we can do in facing up to it would be to try to understand how necessity could possibly be explained in a way that overcomes the disappointment.

4

Value

Thoughts and beliefs to the effect that some things are good and others bad or that one way of acting is better than another are pervasive in human thought. They are questions of value or of evaluation. I do not mean only ethical considerations or questions of right or wrong or of moral value or worth. That is part of it, but I have in mind any positive or negative evaluation of any course of action on any grounds whatsoever. Such judgments are central and indispensable because questions of choice, preference, and reasons for action and belief are central to human life.

We are agents. We do the things we do for certain reasons. And we understand the actions of others by recognizing the reasons for which they do what they do. That is essential to understanding something that happens as an action done intentionally and not simply as a physical movement in space. Understanding movements in the physical world as actions requires recognizing them as done out of a certain intention or for the sake of something or other. Someone raises a glass to take a drink, not to bend the arm in precisely the arc in which it moves; someone speaks in order to tell someone something, not to exercise the vocal chords or break the silence, both of which also happen.

This means that agents who act for reasons cannot be completely indifferent as between all possible courses of action available to them. They intend in their actions to bring about something rather than something else. In acting to bring something about they typically see something in favor of doing it, or prefer it, or want to do it more than its available alternatives. In acting as she does an agent could also be said to take the course of action she favors to be of more value than others, or to evaluate it more highly, or to see more reason to do it. I take these descriptions to be different ways of drawing attention to the 'favoritism' or lack of indifference that must be present among the attitudes an agent of intentional action takes to different aspects of the world in acting as she does.

It is possible for an agent to be completely undecided as between two alternatives on a particular occasion: to find something in favor of each, but no more reason to do one than to do the other.[1] If she then does one of them simply because doing one or the other is better than doing nothing, what she does is not something she finds a reason to do without having equal reason to do the other. The agent does what she does intentionally, but in that special case not because she sees something more in favor of it than in favor of the other. With respect to what she has most reason to do, she finds it is a draw. But someone can be in such a position only by having some evaluative attitudes or other, so even this case does not threaten the idea that holding some evaluative attitudes is essential to the possibility of intentional action.

That 'lack of indifference' that is needed for intentional action is also present in thought and belief without overt action. We come to believe something by finding something we take to be reason to believe it—something we take to count in favor of its truth, or to count more than other considerations we are also aware of. To regard something as reason to believe something is to have an evaluative attitude toward it. We evaluate certain things positively (or more positively) as reason to believe such-and-such. Coming to believe something is in that way something we are 'responsible' for in the sense that our doing it depends on our assessment or evaluation of the strength of the reasons for it. Coming to believe something is not an action we can perform at will, for no reason; to make sense of someone as believing such-and-such we must understand the person to take something or other to be reason to believe it.

There is no suggestion that such assessments or evaluations that are essential to belief and action take the form of an agent's explicitly formulating some such evaluative thoughts "before the mind." The presence of the attitudes is shown in what the person says and does, and in what it takes to make sense of someone as believing such-and-such or doing something or other intentionally. The evaluative attitudes present in both belief and action are what T. M. Scanlon calls "judgement-sensitive attitudes."[2] They involve taking certain considerations to be reason to hold certain

---

1. E.g., Buridan's ass confronted with two equally attractive piles of hay.
2. I am indebted to Scanlon's highly illuminating account of these attitudes and their role in thought and action. See his *What We Owe to Each Other*, Harvard University Press, Cambridge, Mass., 1998, esp. ch. 1.

attitudes: reason to believe or to deny something, reason to prefer or to want or to seek something, reason to intend or to decide or to do something.

There is no question that we all have evaluative attitudes like this, and perhaps that we could not live without them. But there is a very widespread and firmly held metaphysical conviction that what those attitudes are concerned with—what is good or best for someone to do or what there is reason in favor of or against doing—depends always on the wants or desires or feelings or other attitudes of some or all of the people involved. It can seem obvious that there simply could not be any evaluative states of affairs in the world independently of people having certain feelings or taking certain attitudes toward the way things are.

This is a negative metaphysical verdict about the independent reality of values. Like the other negative metaphysical verdicts we have considered, it implies that either such evaluative attitudes are not simply beliefs that something or other is so or, if they are, they are not beliefs that are true of the world as it is independently of what feelings, desires, responses, or thoughts human beings have about it. The verdict says that nothing has any positive or negative value of any kind considered independently of anyone's having such "subjective" psychological responses or attitudes. In the world independent of our having any such attitudes, there is no such thing as one thing's being better or more desirable than another, no such thing as there being more reason to do one thing than to do something else, and no such thing as something's being preferable to other things.

This view can seem simply undeniable. What is the source of the conviction with which it is held? What reasons are there to accept it? This is the first question to ask about this metaphysical verdict. The question has not always been pursued very earnestly or pressed very far. By now the "subjectivity" of all value is widely regarded as no more controversial than the platitude that beauty lies only in the eye of the beholder.[3] We have found reason even in that case to ask how any such metaphysical conclusion is to be reached.

---

3. The verdict that nothing has any value independently of people's desires and interests is not to be understood as the claim that the satisfaction of people's desires and interests is the only thing of positive value there is in the world. That is not a completely general denial of the independent existence of all value; it says that certain states of affairs are good or of value, and it tells us which states of affairs those are. To understand 'Nothing is of value independently of the satisfaction of people's desires and interests' in that way would be like understanding 'Beauty lies only in the eye of the beholder' to say that the only beautiful things there are in the world are beholders' eyes, or 'Necessity is something that exists in the mind, not in objects' to say that there are necessary connections between things that happen in the mind but not in other objects (see p. 21 above).

As with judgments of beauty, one can be struck by widespread differences among individual people and across different cultures and historical periods about the desirability or reasonableness of acting in certain ways. But differences alone, however obvious they might be, are not decisive on the metaphysical question. That people differ, and differ seriously, in what they believe is no reason in itself to conclude that there is nothing in the independent world corresponding to what those different people believe. Their differences can often be explained by their relations to and attitudes about what is actually so in the world they apparently differ about.

If differences alone were what mattered, it looks as if we would have good reason to resist a completely general negative verdict about all values, since there are many evaluations or reasons for action that all people appear to agree about. Nourishment, shelter, security, strength, intelligence, courage, cooperativeness, resourcefulness, and loyalty are likely to be sought for or positively valued everywhere, and hunger, pain, deprivation, aggression, murder, deception, stupidity, and weakness are likely to be equally widely avoided or condemned.

A metaphysical verdict about value does not rest simply on whatever differences in fact exist among people's actual evaluative attitudes. The thesis is metaphysical: it implies that even if everyone shared all the same evaluative opinions or attitudes there would still be nothing in the world independently of their holding those attitudes for them to be evaluatively right or wrong about. This also means that if people differ on evaluative questions, as they seem to, they do not thereby contradict one another about anything evaluative. According to the negative metaphysical verdict, there is neither conflict nor accord about anything evaluative that holds in the independent world. The thesis is metaphysical in purporting to tell us what that independent world is like and thereby to explain the relation between people's evaluative attitudes and what is so in that world, whatever those attitudes happen to be.

The acceptability of a negative metaphysical thesis about value therefore depends on achieving a conception of what is so in a fully independent world while at the same time showing that our evaluative judgments state nothing that is so in that world. But any account worth taking seriously must give an accurate description of the evaluative judgments we actually make. In other cases we have encountered obstacles to arriving at a metaphysically 'purified' view of this kind that we can consistently accept.

To acknowledge that people hold evaluative attitudes at all we must recognize the contents of the evaluative attitudes we ascribe to others in making sense of them as acting in the ways they do. One way to try to do that would be to construct the contents of those attitudes out of whatever purely non-evaluative materials are thought to be available. That would require a reduction or equivalence of the contents of evaluative attitudes to something expressed in purely non-evaluative terms. We found good reason to doubt that that can be done for the modal ideas of causal dependence and 'absolute' necessity. But even if in this case a non-evaluative equivalence could be found for each evaluative attitude, would the ascription of such attitudes, so understood, make sense of agents acting for reasons in the right way? That is one question.

Without such a reduction, could one accept a negative metaphysical verdict about value and still recognize the distinctively evaluative contents of the attitudes one must attribute to agents to make sense of their actions? Could someone who has eliminated all evaluation from his own conception of the world even recognize any such attitudes at all? That is another question. Difficulties of this general shape have arisen before, and we have found no reason for optimism about overcoming them.

This second and perhaps more troubling question raises the doubt whether someone who claims to hold no evaluative opinions could even try to carry out a metaphysical investigation of the status of value. It is difficult to see how any thinker could avoid making evaluative judgments about one thing's counting in favor of or being a reason to believe something else. To think consecutively at all, we must take something we already know or accept as reason to believe or think something else. If that is an evaluative attitude, and if having some such attitudes is unavoidable in thinking and believing, this would leave someone who denies the metaphysical reality of all values in an apparently inescapable inconsistency. It would be like the inconsistency involved in trying to deny the metaphysical reality of causation while offering an unmasking causal explanation of how people come to believe in causation. The conclusion that there is no such relation in the independent world could be 'reached' in that way only by someone who accepts something that the conclusion he accepts denies.

All this perhaps suggests that evaluative attitudes of some kind are as pervasive and as indispensable to all thought and action—and so as resistant to completely general metaphysical unmasking—as beliefs about necessity and perhaps causal dependence have also revealed themselves to be. But I think it is easy to feel unmoved by these potential obstacles, or even to feel that the metaphysical reflection in which they arise is not really needed to reach a negative conclusion about the independence of value. It can be felt to be obvious and undeniable without further discussion that a negative verdict about the independent reality of value simply must be right.

The merest reflection on our thoughts about one thing's being better than another, or on something's being the thing to do or not to do, can seem to be enough to bring home to us the truth of this negative verdict. For specifically moral judgments about something's being good or bad, right or wrong, or virtuous or vicious, Hume offered this simple invitation:

> Take any action allow'd to be vicious: Wilful murder, for instance. Examine it in all lights, and see if you can find that matter of fact, or real existence, which you call *vice*. In which-ever way you take it, you find only certain passions, motives, volitions and thoughts. There is no other matter of fact in the case. The vice entirely escapes you, as long as you consider the object.[4]

The 'object' here is the act that you judge to be vicious or evil. The claim is that among all the properties that belong to that act independently of your making that judgment about it, there is no viciousness or evil. There is no such 'matter of fact' in the independent world so understood.

This is a dramatic expression of one instance of the completely general negative metaphysical verdict about value. It is strikingly parallel to Hume's denial of any necessary connection to be found in a particular instance of what we take to be a case of cause and effect. Hume's position on the non-independence of values has been even more widely accepted down the centuries than his conclusions about causation. But, as in that case, this is a particular illustration of his metaphysical view, not in itself a persuasive reason to accept that metaphysical verdict in the first place.

It is true that an act of willful murder can be examined or considered in many different "lights" or in many different ways without our finding its viciousness or evil. We might think of the act only as a series of movements, for instance, or only as something that happened on a Tuesday. We might consider it only as the comings and goings of certain passions, motives, volitions, and thoughts. There would be nothing in those ways of thinking of the act that would enable us to find it vicious or evil. But Hume says that even if we examine the act "in all lights," or under all ways of thinking of it, we will not find the viciousness of the act in "the object." But that appears not to be so. If we examine the act in the "light" of its moral qualities—whether it is vicious and evil or not—we will find that it *is* vicious and evil; it is an act of willful murder, after all. So it seems that considering the act in light of *every* possible way we can take things to be would lead us to find the viciousness or evil of the act to be part of the way things are.

---

4. D. Hume, *A Treatise of Human Nature* (ed. L. A. Selby-Bigge), Oxford University Press, Oxford, 1978, pp. 468–469.

It is true that this act's being vicious is not something we could ever find in it if we had already arrived at a metaphysically 'purified' conception that describes the world without the evaluative terms of morality, or perhaps without evaluative terms at all. We would already have reached the conclusion that non-evaluative matters of fact are the only matters of fact there are. That is how Hume knows we will never find the viciousness or evil in the act; it is not there. But metaphysical reflection is needed to lead us to that conception of the world and so to reveal that negative conclusion to us. We start that process of reflection with everything we believe or accept or endorse; where else are we to start? So we start the reflection with the thought, among other things, that that act of willful murder is vicious or evil. That is something we believe to be true of that "object," even if we can eventually be led to a more austere and metaphysically 'purified' conception of an independent world. By what process of reflection can we be led from that starting-point to that conclusion?

Hume says that in the search for "that matter of fact, or real existence, which you call vice,"

> You never can find it, till you turn your reflection into your own breast, and find a sentiment of disapprobation, which arises in you, towards the action. Here is a matter of fact, but it is an object of feeling, not of reason.[5]

Hume thinks of that "sentiment of disapprobation" as a certain kind of feeling or passion. You call the act vicious or evil because of the way you feel about it, not because you have reached the conclusion that it is vicious or evil by reasoning about the way things are.

When generalized to all of morality, this is the view that there is a feeling or sentiment involved in the making of every moral judgment. A full account of moral thought would have to identify that special kind of feeling and describe it more fully. Hume calls the feeling "disagreeable" in the case of vice and "agreeable" in the case of virtue, but that is obviously not enough to identify it. Not everything that produces a disagreeable or an agreeable feeling is regarded as vicious or as virtuous. It must also be explained what role that special kind of feeling plays in the moral judgment. Making a judgment that the act is vicious or evil could not be simply announcing the presence of that feeling in one's consciousness. That would not be a moral or evaluative judgment, but simply the announcement of a certain kind of non-moral or non-evaluative

---

5. Ibid., p. 469.

matter of fact. Nor could the moral judgment be thought of as only a statement about the kinds of feelings the speaker and all or most other people do or would get from an act of that kind. That too would be a non-evaluative judgment of a certain matter of fact. It is something that could be found to be true (or false) by observation and reasoning about the way things are. But Hume thinks moral conclusions are not arrived at by that kind of reasoning.

Even if you do find in yourself a "sentiment of disapprobation" toward an act of wilful murder that you judge to be vicious or evil, you do not find in that feeling or "sentiment" itself any viciousness or evil. Your "sentiment" is directed toward that act, and in having or feeling that "sentiment" toward it you regard the act as vicious, as something to be disapproved of, and you accordingly disapprove of it (to put it mildly). But if you do regard the act in that way, you thereby ascribe viciousness or evil to the act, take it to be part of the way things are that the act is vicious or evil and is to be disapproved of.

The metaphysical verdict denies that there are any such matters of fact in the world. It implies that the way you take things to be in making the judgment that the act is vicious is not any way things are in the independent world. The verdict does not deny that you feel a certain "sentiment" of disapprobation toward the act, or that you ascribe the moral qualities of viciousness or evil to it. But it denies that there is anything in the act corresponding to that feeling or to what you thereby ascribe to it.

> Vice and virtue, therefore, may be compar'd to sounds, colours, heat and cold, which, according to modern philosophy, are not qualities in objects, but perceptions in the mind.[6]

If the metaphysical conclusion that there are only non-moral or perhaps non-evaluative matters of fact in the world had already been reached, this is the kind of view of vice and virtue that would have to be accepted. On that view, whatever qualities of 'vice' or 'virtue' or 'to-be-disapproved of' we might ascribe to actions in our evaluative judgments, they could not be qualities of the acts or objects to which we ascribe them. There would be no moral or evaluative matters of fact in the world to make such judgments true or false. It is because Hume thinks of the independent world in that non-evaluative way that he thinks moral or evaluative judgments cannot be understood as statements about how things are in that world, just as he thinks judgments about the colors or sounds of things cannot be understood as correctly describing the

---

6. Ibid., pp. 468–469.

independent world. The metaphysical conception of the world supported by what Hume calls "the modern philosophy" is a world completely devoid of color and sound and value.

Before a clear conception of an exclusively non-evaluative world of this kind has been reached, and even in the reflections that are meant to lead to it, we must be sure that the evaluative attitudes the metaphysical project subjects to scrutiny are the ways we actually think in making such judgments. This raises the second of the three questions to be pressed about any such metaphysical verdict: can what it says or implies about our actual ways of thinking be seen to be correct? Are the evaluative judgments we make about one thing's being better than another, or a certain consideration's counting in favor of doing such-and-such, judgments or beliefs as to how things are?

The main reason usually offered for thinking evaluative judgments cannot be understood in that way is precisely what we have seen to be characteristic of evaluative attitudes: accepting them has motivational force. The idea is that beliefs in (mere) matters of fact in the world have no such practical force or efficacy on their own. Hume puts the point almost syllogistically.

> Morals excite passions and produce or prevent actions.
> Reason of itself is utterly impotent in this particular.
> The rules of morality, therefore, are not conclusions of our reason.[7]

This argument as it stands is valid. By reason here Hume means the discovery of truth and falsehood,[8] and its outcome is belief. If all beliefs or "conclusions of reason" are incapable in themselves of generating action, but "morals," or the evaluative attitudes we accept in accepting "the rules of morality," do have motivational effect, then those attitudes are not beliefs as to what is so in the world. The point could presumably be generalized to include all evaluative attitudes, not only those concerned with morals.

But is it true that beliefs are incapable in themselves of generating action? Or that all beliefs are beliefs only in non-evaluative matters of fact? Again, that is something we could be forced to accept if we had already arrived at a completely non-moral or non-evaluative conception of the world. But we still have not found sufficient reason to draw that conclusion. It can be granted that belief in a non-evaluative matter of fact can leave one completely indifferent to that fact. To hold a belief of

---

7. Ibid., p. 457.
8. Ibid., p. 458.

that kind is consistent with having no preference, no desire, and no evaluative attitude one way or the other toward what is so. Holding such a belief would therefore have no effect in itself on one's actions or on one's reasons to act. That is what Hume thinks the "discoveries" of "cold," "indifferent" "reason" are like.[9]

It can also be granted that in holding an evaluative attitude toward something one is *not* completely indifferent to it; "favoritism" or lack of indifference toward something one takes to be so involves at least an inclination to act in a certain way. Someone who has no inclination to act in a certain way, or who seldom or never acts that way in the appropriate circumstances, could not be said to favor or to positively evaluate acting in that way in those circumstances. Being inclined to act in a certain way is not necessarily to act in that way; one might also have evaluative attitudes that oppose acting in that way. But those competing attitudes and inclinations all involve not being completely indifferent to acting in that way. They bear in one way or another on one's reason for doing something.

All this is true of acting for reasons and of the evaluative attitudes essential to it. But it does not follow from all this that holding an evaluative attitude cannot be understood as believing or acknowledging or taking something or other to be so. If something's being so (or not) is a matter of fact, it has not been shown that evaluative attitudes cannot be understood as beliefs in, or acknowledgments of, evaluative matters of fact. It is widely held that there could be no such thing as 'an evaluative matter of fact.'[10] But if that is supported only by the thought that a fact is something that is said to be so by a non-evaluative sentence that is true, proper understanding of our evaluative judgments could give us reason to reject such a restrictive definition.

J. L. Mackie defended a version of the view that there are no evaluative matters of fact. He denied that there are any "objective values" in ethics on the grounds that if there were, they would be "entities or qualities or relations of a very strange sort, utterly different from anything else in the universe" and could be known only by "some special faculty of moral perception . . . utterly different from our ordinary ways of knowing everything else."[11] If this means only that ethical judgments (or evaluative

---

9. Ibid., e.g., p. 414.

10. We noted similar resistance to the idea of 'necessary matters of fact,' but without finding a convincing source of the resistance. See pp. 68–69 above.

11. J. L. Mackie, *Ethics: Inventing Right and Wrong*, Penguin, Harmondsworth, England, 1977, p. 38.

judgments generally) are different from judgments of all other kinds, and that our awareness or acceptance of them is different from our ways of knowing all other kinds of truths, there would be no reason to disagree. Everything is what it is and not another thing.

But Mackie stresses what he calls the "queerness" of all such alleged entities or states of affairs or matters of fact. If evaluative judgments have motivational force, he thinks knowledge of what I have called an evaluative matter of fact would "provide the knower with both a direction and an overriding[12] motive; something's being good both tells the person who knows this to pursue it and makes him pursue it. . . . the end has to-be-pursuedness somehow built into it."[13] And he thinks there is no way to explain how this could be so.

Mackie's description does perhaps make acknowledging an evaluative state of affairs sound odd, but there is nothing odd or "queer" in the familiar fact of a person seeing something to be so and seeing it to be reason to act in a certain way and so being moved to act in that way. Someone sees a friend in distress, for instance. She sees the distress of the friend, and she takes that distress as a reason to do something to help, and is moved to act accordingly. Given these facts, we could even say, in Mackie's words, that the friend's distress "tells" the person to "pursue the end" of easing the distress and so "makes" her pursue it. Of course, she is not "made" to do it in the way a stern master might tell someone to do something and even make him do it. It is because the agent holds the attitudes she does about distress, or her friend's distress, that it indicates to her what should be done, and she is moved to act. She sees the distress as a reason to help relieve it; she evaluates her friend's distress negatively and seeks to eliminate it. It could even be said, in Mackie's fanciful words, that for this person on this occasion the elimination of her friend's distress "has to-be-pursuedness somehow built into it." But there is nothing fanciful in someone's believing and acting on the belief that her friend's distress is reason to help, or that her friend's relief from distress is something to be pursued.

Mackie objects to this way of understanding evaluative judgments because he thinks the alleged knowledge or belief or awareness cannot be explained in the way our knowledge of all the non-evaluative things

---

12. Mackie presumably calls the motive overriding because he is concerned with the question of what is the right thing to do, in which he thinks the answer should be overriding. But that need not be so with evaluative attitudes in general; they need not be ethical or moral or overriding or decisive.

13. Mackie, *Ethics*, p. 40.

we know can be explained. Again, if this is to have any force, it must amount to more than the observation that acceptance of evaluative judgments is different in certain respects from acceptance of other kinds of judgments. Mackie's "epistemological" objection to "objective values" is that "none of our ordinary accounts of sensory perception or . . . the framing and confirming of explanatory hypotheses or inference" can explain how we can be aware of these allegedly evaluative states of affairs.[14] How strong an objection this turns out to be depends on how well the "ordinary" ways of explaining knowledge that Mackie has in mind can account for even the "ordinary" knowledge of non-evaluative matters of fact that we know we have.

Mackie envisages an explanation of human knowledge based on what he calls purely "empiricist foundations." But such an account, even if we had one, would be less than conclusive on the metaphysical question. We saw that the restrictive "empiricist" conceptions of perception and knowledge that were meant to support comparable denials of the metaphysical reality of causation and of 'absolute' necessity left no room for knowledge of either of those modalities, thereby appearing to leave their presence in the world dubious at best. But that was no stronger a reason to deny the existence of such modal connections in the independent world than it was to deny the adequacy of the restrictive conception of knowledge that implies they could never be known. The conflict in those cases was even good reason to deny those epistemological doctrines, given the apparent indispensability of causal dependence and 'absolute' necessity for any thought or knowledge of the world at all.

It is sometimes suggested that what is distinctive and less than "objective" about evaluative attitudes and opinions is that they are acquired and maintained only through a process of socialization into the practice and the associated values prevalent in a particular culture. That is true, but it is true of all our concepts and ways of thinking, and so of the possibility of our knowing anything about the world. That there are objects of certain kinds in the world around us, that they have been there for some time, that they stand in causal relations to one another and to us, that some things hold with necessity and could not possibly have been otherwise: all this we know only because we have acquired the conceptual and linguistic resources made available by our culture that enable us to know such things. But that does not show that the truth of what we come to know in any of those ways depends on anyone's engaging in

14. Ibid., p. 39.

the practices that make it possible for us to come to know it. Nor does a parallel conclusion follow about our evaluative beliefs and attitudes.

I think there is something deeper behind the idea that evaluative attitudes with motivational force are not to be understood as judgments to the effect that something or other is so. There is at work a certain conception of desire and motivation and action. Wants or desires on the part of the agent are necessary for intentional action, and it is felt that they could not play that role if they were judgments or opinions to the effect that something or other is so, especially judgments that something evaluative is so.[15]

For all its apparent appeal, it is difficult to make this line of thinking both fully explicit and plausible. It starts from the undeniable thought that the person who finds her friend in distress acts as she does because she *wants* to do something to help him, and that she would not act that way, whatever she believed, if she did not have the relevant want or desire. Added to this is the further thought that a person can believe or acknowledge or judge that it is a good thing to help this friend here right now, or that there is good reason to do it, but still not act to help the friend despite holding those beliefs. Both these things can be true of a person and an act. The conclusion that I think is meant to be drawn from them is that the motivational force in the person's being led to act therefore cannot come simply from the person's judgment or belief or acknowledgment that such-and-such is good or is a reason to act in a certain way. The idea is that since belief in or acknowledgment of a reason to act *can* fail to lead to action, there must be some want or desire, or at least something in addition to the person's acceptance of such-and-such as being so, that is needed to produce the action.

This felt need for such an additional factor can make it look as if the wants or desires necessary for action must therefore be understood as something like feelings or passions or at least urges that are not themselves beliefs. That is why Hume thought that not all the attitudes that lead us to act can be "conclusions of our reason." Some "feelings" or "sentiments" or "passions" are needed. It is precisely because moral 'judgments' can lead to action that he thought they could not be "conclusions of our reason." So "Morality is more properly felt, than judg'd of."[16]

---

15. On these matters I have found Scanlon, *What We Owe*, ch. 1, especially helpful. See also W. Quinn, "Putting Rationality in Its Place," in his *Morality and Action*, Cambridge University Press, Cambridge, 1993, and G. F. Schueler, *Desire*, MIT Press, Cambridge, Mass., 1995.

16. Hume, *Treatise*, p. 470.

I think the conclusion that desires must be understood as feelings or passions or urges that provide separate motivational force leading to action is not supported by this reasoning. Furthermore, if such a separate motivational item were needed, it could not really account for intentional action in the right way. On the first point, it is true that someone can take something to be a reason, even a very strong reason, to act in a certain way and then not act in that way for that reason when the time comes. But it does not follow that when someone does act in the appropriate way on the basis of what he takes to be good reason to do it, some additional motivational item beyond that evaluative belief was needed to "help" produce the action. No separate feeling or urge of that kind need be present.[17]

One way to see this is to consider first a person's coming to *believe* something on the basis of something he takes to be reason to believe it. A person wondering whether it is true that q might find that it is true that p. If he takes that to be good reason to believe that q he can then immediately come to believe that q. The transition is immediate in the sense that it need not be understood as his passing through an intermediate step of first accepting the proposition 'p is reason to believe that q' and then combining it with his acceptance of 'p' to constitute an augmented reason for believing that q. If acceptance of all the propositions making up such an augmented reason was always needed for a thinker to arrive at one belief by reasoning from another, then an even more augmented reason would always be needed in moving reasonably from whatever propositions had been accepted so far to any desired conclusion. On that assumption, no conclusion could ever be reached on the basis of reasons or reasoning.[18]

This shows that a person who comes to believe that p, which he takes to be reason to believe that q, can be led by having those two attitudes to believe that q. It is true that the person might not have come to believe that q even though he believes that p and regards p as good reason to believe that q. He might have been aware of stronger reasons against believing that q, despite his accepting that p. But on this occasion, in the absence of any such overriding reasons, his believing that p and his

---

17. I objected to Hume's account of action and desire on these grounds in my *Hume*, Routledge and Kegan Paul, London, 1977. I would no longer endorse the crude positive account of desire I suggested there.

18. See Lewis Carroll, "What the Tortoise Said to Achilles," *Mind* 1895. This is not to deny that the person described could be said to believe each of those intermediate propositions. I discuss some of the implications of Carroll's argument for the understanding of belief in "Inference, Belief, and Understanding," *Mind* 1979.

judgment or acknowledgment that p is reason to believe that q are enough to lead him to believe that q.

Someone who regularly proceeds in this way, who comes to believe things on the basis of what he regards as good or the best reason to believe them, is a competent reasoner or inquirer. He learns to exercise good judgment in the assessment of reasons for belief and to adjust his beliefs accordingly. He gets a good sense of what is reason to believe what. A person like that will come to believe what he finds there is reason to believe simply by finding what he regards as reasons to believe it. We make sense of such a person's believing the things he does by finding that he comes to believe them on the basis of what he takes to be reasons to believe them. Of course, a reasonable person does not believe everything for which he finds he has some reason, and he might occasionally not believe something even though he believes he has the best or strongest reason to believe it. He might have unresolved suspicions or doubts that he cannot fully articulate or support with equally strong reasons on the other side that leave him reluctant to conclude what he nonetheless concedes his best reasons at the moment clearly support. This can be a virtue in a careful, sensitive reasoner.

All this is true of a competent reasoner or inquirer: someone who is inclined or disposed to come to believe things in this "reason-based" way when he finds what he takes to be good reason to believe them. It is difficult if not impossible to understand how someone who lacked the inclinations or dispositions of such a competent reasoner could come to believe anything at all, or could come to believe something on the basis of something else. Even if such a person could be understood to believe something on a particular occasion, and to have come to believe something else, it would not explain his coming to the second belief to say only that he came to believe yet a third proposition: that what he first believed is good reason to believe the second. For a person lacking the appropriate inclinations or disposition, that would be just a third, further belief that he 'accepts' in the same way he was thought to 'accept' the other two. His 'acceptance' of that third belief would not so far explain his coming to have the second belief given that he has the first, any more than his having the first belief was enough to explain his coming to believe the second. Some further explanation would still be needed of why he came to have that second belief. Obviously the addition of more and more beliefs that he 'accepts' about one thing's being reason to believe another would not help. This is the lesson of Lewis Carroll's paradox.

For a competent reasoner with a settled inclination to believe something when he believes something he recognizes to be reason to believe it, no additional explanation would be needed. It is not that what is present in the competent reasoner but absent in the 'incompetent' believer is some mental item or feeling or urge that carries the competent reasoner with "belief-inducing force" from one thing he accepts to another. The only difference between the two is the presence or absence of a settled general inclination or disposition to come to believe things on the basis of what one takes to be reason to believe them. No further motivational item with some such "belief-inducing force" is needed. And if some such item were needed to generate a person's belief, given that he believes something else, the person would not come to believe what he does on the basis of something he takes to be reason to believe it. He would have been led to it by the "force" exerted on him.

The case of intentional action or acting for a reason is parallel in this respect. The person who finds her friend in distress and is the kind of person who in general responds to her friend's distress with offers to help will in general act to help her friend when she sees it is called for. She might not always do it, especially if on a particular occasion she also recognizes other constraints with greater strength that lead her to do something else. But when she does help, she does it because she takes it that help is called for, that the distress is reason to act in a certain way— and because she is the kind of person who in general acts in that way when it is called for. So her having the inclination or disposition, or her being the kind of person she is in those respects, is all it takes, once the distress has been recognized, for her to act in that way in the absence of anything she takes to be overriding reasons against it.

Someone who did not have such a general inclination or disposition could not be said to recognize or acknowledge a friend's distress as a reason to help. Those who claim to have such an admirable attitude but seldom or never act on it in the appropriate circumstances would raise doubts about whether they really do regard a friend's distress as reason to help. If someone helps a friend in distress on one occasion but does not have any general inclination or disposition to do things like that for that reason, there would be a question of why the person acted as he did that time. Further explanation would be called for. But any further explanation that made the action intelligible would appeal to some considerations or other that the agent took to be reasons to act in that way. The sudden appearance of an additional motivational feeling or urge with "action-inducing force" would not explain his doing what he did intentionally.

There is a strong tendency to resist this way of understanding action. It rests on a conception of wants or desires according to which they are the *origin* of all action and so the *source* of an agent's having any reason to act in a certain way. Wants and desires are understood as the source and explanation of motivation in the sense that an action is explained by the agent's seeking satisfaction of the wants or desires that give rise to it. The thought is that it is only because the person who helps her friend in distress *wants* to help him, or *wants* to be or to be thought of as a certain kind of person, or *wants* something else that she thinks acting that way will bring, that she has or takes herself to have a reason to help him. The idea is that if she had no such want or desire she would not take herself to have reason, and so would have no reason to help.

I think some such view of wants or desires and their role in action lies at the heart of the widespread acceptance of a negative metaphysical verdict about values. I believe this view can be shown to rest on a confusion about reasons for action. But even if the view is accepted, it offers no prospect of explaining intentional action in the right way. Again a comparison with believing something for a reason can help bring this out. Someone who believes that *p* and takes *p* to be reason to believe that *q*, and so believes that *q* for that reason, could be said to believe that *q* *because* he believes that *p*. His believing that *p* is what explains his coming to believe that *q*. It could even be said that *the reason* he believes that *q* is that he believes that *p*. But that does not mean that the person's reason for believing that *q* is *his believing* that *p*. Nor is his reason for believing that *q* *his taking p* to be reason to believe it. His reason, and what he takes to be reason to believe that *q*, is *p*.

A person's being in the state of *believing* something or other has in general very little or nothing to do with whether the person has reason to believe something else.[19] What matters for that question for the agent is whether the belief in question is true, or whether there is good reason to believe it, not simply whether the person *believes* it is true or *believes* that there is good reason to believe it. If someone accepts the conclusion of a mathematical proof, for instance, it is not the person's *believing* the premises and the validity of the intervening steps that he takes to be reason to believe the conclusion; the premises and the validity of the

---

19. It is possible to imagine unusual cases of this. Someone might take his believing something to be reason for him to believe that at some time in the past he found something in favor of that belief. But if, in general, a person's *believing* that *p* is thought of as a person's reason to believe that *q*, at least when *p* implies *q* and the person knows that it does, then a person's *believing* that *p* would be reason for the person to believe that *p*, since *p* implies *p* and the person knows that it does. Merely believing something would be reason to believe that it is true. See Niko Kolodny, "Why Be Rational?" *Mind* 2005.

steps themselves are his reason. A person's believing the premises and the validity of the steps has nothing in general to do with whether the conclusion he believes is true.[20] He could be said to believe the conclusion *because* he takes the premises he accepts to be reason to believe it, but his *taking* that to be so is not his reason. What he takes to be reason does not involve his believing or taking any attitude to anything. The premises and the steps he accepts as his reason say nothing about anyone believing anything.

Similarly, if someone takes a friend's distress as reason to help him, her reason for acting in that way is the distress, or what is bad about it, not her taking the distress to be bad or as a reason to help. We could say that she acts as she does '*because* she takes that as a reason,' that her taking that as a reason is '*what explains* her acting as she does,' or even that '*the reason* she acts as she does' is that she takes the distress to be a reason to help. In that way, her taking that attitude to the distress comes into the explanation of her doing what she does. But her *taking* a certain consideration to be reason to act in a certain way is not her reason to act in that way. It is the consideration itself to which she takes that attitude—the distress, or its badness—that she takes to be a reason. Her being the kind of person who is moved to act by her friend's distress also comes into the explanation of her doing what she does. She acts that way *because* she is that kind of person. But the fact that she is that kind of person is not part of her reason for helping her friend either. What she takes to be reason to help is her friend's distress, not what kind of person she herself is.

It can be said that such a person *wants* to help her friend in distress, or even that she helps him because she wants to. She sees that he is in distress, she takes the distress as reason to help, and she is the kind of person who is moved by that recognition to act in that way. But her wanting to do it, or her wanting the end of her friend's distress, is not a feeling or passion or urge that is the *source* of her having reason to help him or of her taking the distress to be reason to help him. Her wanting to help him is a matter of her seeing something in favor of doing it and being the kind of person who is moved to act by what she recognizes to be reason to act in that way. Her wanting to act in that way could be said to be the source or origin of her action in the sense that it is what leads

---

20. Except perhaps for those of such impressive intellects that their believing something is in itself some reason to think it is true. There are those who appear to regard some of their beliefs in this way.

her to act as she does, once she knows about the distress. But her having the want that plays that role in her action involves her making a judgment about the value or worth of doing a certain thing, or about there being reason to do it. And that evaluative judgment or opinion is not an evaluation made relative to her wanting something or other. It does not have its 'source' or 'origin' in a want or desire understood as something different from acceptance or endorsement of a judgment about the value or worth of doing a certain thing.

This can appear not to be so with what are sometimes called simple or basic wants or desires. A person is thirsty and wants a drink, so he crosses the street in order to get one. His wanting a drink is the source or origin of his action in the sense that it is what explains his crossing the street when and where he does, or is the reason why he does it. But his wanting a drink, even in that case, involves his seeing something in favor of having a drink—his regarding relief from thirst, for instance, as something he favors or sees as worth having now. That evaluation is the source or origin of his action. To say that the source or basis of that evaluative attitude must be some want or desire such as a desire for relief from thirst changes nothing. If the person wants relief from thirst, he attaches some value to it or sees something in favor of it; being thirsty for too long is unpleasant, for instance. To say that therefore there must be a basic want or desire for pleasure or the absence of unpleasantness at the source or basis of his positive evaluation of relief from thirst again changes nothing. His action of crossing the street is explained as an intentional action only if the explanation implies that he took relief from thirst or the pleasure to be got from it, or at least some characteristic or consequence of the action that he was in favor of or regarded as desirable, as reason to act as he did.

This is present in the very idea of the *satisfaction* of a desire. A desire is satisfied when what it is a desire for is realized or achieved. If an action is to be explained by the agent's seeking satisfaction of the desires that lead him to act, there must be some determinate desire, and so some determinate satisfaction, that the agent seeks. To say only that he acts because he seeks satisfaction of his desires leaves it unspecified what he wants, and so what would satisfy the desires he has. It would explain nothing. To want something, or to seek a certain satisfaction, is (at the very least) to assess positively the condition that would satisfy that want. The agent sees or takes there to be something in favor of or something desirable or worth having or achieving in the state of affairs in which his desire would be satisfied. Desires or wants that could explain intentional action must be understood as possessing this kind of intentionality.

The point is brought out by Warren Quinn's striking example of someone with a strong but apparently unintelligible urge to turn on radios.[21] The man is said to see nothing in turning on radios and not to favor or evaluate positively in any way their being on. He does not seek the music or news or commercial advertising he gets when he turns them on. He does not pursue the goal of having every radio in the world turned on. But he more or less irresistibly moves to turn on every radio he sees. Quinn's main point with the example is that this man cannot be said to have a desire to turn on radios. We cannot explain his turning on a particular radio by saying he wanted to turn it on, or saw something in its being turned on. With that evaluative element missing, we cannot understand him as intentionally turning on the radio.

Further reflection on the case leads to further puzzlement, but without obscuring the main point. Could someone regularly and deliberately reach out and push a button or turn a knob without doing so intentionally? Could one do so intentionally with the aim of turning on the radio even though one sees nothing in favor of the radio's being turned on? Habitual directed action normally betokens acknowledgment or pursuit of something to which one attaches some value. No such thing is meant to be present in this case. Almost irresistible urges normally produce anxiety or unease when they are controlled or repressed. If the man turned on radios in order to relieve the anxiety he feels when he finds them off, his action would be intelligible as intentional after all; he would see something in a radio's being on. With no such explanation his turning on a radio would seem to remain unexplained even though he apparently crosses the room intentionally in order to turn a radio on. What makes the person difficult to understand as we press further is still the difficulty of seeing how what the person does is connected with any wants or desires he can be understood to have. Uncertainty about what he is intentionally or not intentionally doing derives from what is specified from the outset as his lack of any evaluation of radios being on. Because he is to be understood as finding nothing desirable in or in favor of radios being turned on, these questions about his wants or desires remain unanswered.

Hume spoke of the "feelings" or "passions" that give rise to action as "original existences, compleat in themselves," with "no representative quality."[22] That makes them sound like drives or urges we simply find ourselves with that make us move or behave in certain ways. If they

---

21. Quinn, "Putting Rationality in Its Place," pp. 236ff.
22. Hume, *Treatise*, p. 415.

carry with them no specification of any conditions under which they would be satisfied, as desires can be satisfied, intentional actions would not be explained by the presence of such things or by an agent's seeking 'satisfaction' of them. There would be no such thing as satisfaction of them; they would not be wants or desires *for* something. Such forces or urges or passions might produce results, but their presence and their efficacy would make no sense of agents as doing things because there is something they want or seek. Perhaps some such force is at work in the man with the radios. Not every urge or force that makes us do something is a want or desire for something. Forces operating on us can make us sneeze, for instance, or can make us break through the thin ice we are walking on, but we do so with no desire to do so and without doing so intentionally.

The idea of feelings or passions as forces that we simply find ourselves with and that push us into action is encouraged by the traditional rhetoric of a contrast between "reason" and "passion" or "thought" and "feeling." The gap can seem absolute if feelings are regarded as something like sensations with a distinctive felt character and if thought is seen as the cool contemplation of an inert idea 'present to the mind.' But that whole picture is the legacy of an unfortunate "faculty" psychology of the mind left over from the past. Many passions, feelings, and sentiments themselves involve evaluative and other propositional attitudes. Hume's own "sentiment of disapprobation or blame" toward an act of willful murder is a sentiment one could not feel without having an evaluative attitude toward the act, and so thinking of it in a certain way. An evaluative attitude is present in and essential to that feeling or sentiment of disapprobation just as it is involved in a judgment or belief that the act is vicious or evil and worthy of disapproval and blame. Even to feel thirsty or to "feel like having a drink" is to have a positive evaluative attitude toward having a drink. Sometimes when you feel that way your throat might feel dry and at other times you might have a slight headache, but neither of those sensations is a feeling of thirst or a desire for a drink.

The complexities of the kinds of feelings, sentiments, desires, and passions we are capable of are as rich as the different possible ways of describing what a feeling is a feeling of or what would satisfy a particular desire or what a certain passion is a passion for. Evaluative and other propositional attitudes are essential to the identity of a great many of our feelings, sentiments, and passions just as they are to the identity of our judgments or beliefs.

That is not to say in either case that an explicit formulation of some propositional item representing an evaluative state of affairs must somehow appear before or pass through the agent's mind. Wanting and acting and so holding the evaluative attitudes essential to them are natural, spontaneous, un-self-conscious forms of adult human activity and response. Agents can be said to have whatever attitudes make the best sense of their doing what they intentionally say and do. Intentional agents are assumed to be capable of understanding the contents of the attitudes, sentiments, thoughts, and beliefs ascribed to them in explaining those actions. But none of that carries any implication about what actually passes through an agent's mind.

Evaluations are taken into consideration in a person's deliberations about what to do and in the actions that result from them whether those evaluations are part of the person's feelings and sentiments or part of the contents of the person's judgments or beliefs. They play the same role in action in either case. In reflecting on what to do a person can find some of his past evaluations no longer worthy of endorsement, or even that he was wrong in evaluating certain things as he did in the past. This can happen by his getting new non-evaluative information. Someone enjoying herself at a party with friends can take herself to have no reason to leave and every reason to stay and enjoy the fun. She would be wrong about that if the building was on fire. She would acknowledge her error or mis-judgment if she knew about the fire, and she would acknowledge retrospectively that her earlier judgment was wrong. Rejection and alteration of one's evaluative attitudes can also be achieved on evaluative grounds alone. With more careful consideration and reflection on one's earlier evaluations, or with greater awareness of previously overlooked evaluative complexities, or just with growing maturity and sensitivity, one can reject past evaluations in favor of what one now sees to be a better way things should be.

From the point of view of the deliberating agent, then, the evaluative question of what to do or of what one has reason or most reason to do can present itself as something one can be right or wrong about. Someone who asks what she should do now, or what she has most reason to do, asks a question that she regards as having a right or wrong answer, or at least better or worse answers. What is to be deemed 'right' or 'best' here is to be assessed according to the agent's own evaluations, since the agent is the person whose action will be the outcome of the deliberation. But that does not mean that only the agent's current evaluations are to be taken into consideration, since those evaluations can always be revised for what the agent can come to see as good reasons.

Agents who seek advice ask for help with the practical question of what they should do now. For the best advice they should not ask the advisor simply 'What would *you* do in this situation?' but rather 'What should *I* do now?'[23] Advisors who will not have to perform the eventual action can nonetheless consider that same question: what should this person do now? For them too it is a question of what is best; what is the right or best answer, including what are the best evaluations against which the question of what this person should do in this situation is to be settled?

That is a question other people can also discuss and try to answer even if they are not invited to advise the agent. For them too the question presents itself as a question to which there is a right or wrong or at least a better or worse answer. An answer must take into account the information available to the agent and her own evaluations of various considerations, but whether the agent's current information and evaluations should remain as they are or should be altered to give a better answer to the question what she should do is itself part of the evaluative question under consideration by everyone, including the agent.

This again finds a parallel with reasons to believe. Someone who asks himself what he has most reason to believe in a particular situation might take it that *p*, which he believe, gives him strongest reason to believe that *q*. That is something evaluative that he takes to be so, but he could come on further reflection to think that it is not so. He could reject his earlier assessment of his reason either because he gets new information that casts doubt on the strength of *p* as reason to believe that *q* or because he finds his earlier assessment faulty or at least suspicious even without any new non-evaluative facts. Someone else who is asked what that person has most reason to believe in that situation will try to determine what is so in the situation and whether *p*, which the person believes, really gives the person strongest reason to believe that *q*. That is the very question the believer himself asks. It is a question of what is so and of whether what is taken to be reason to believe something is properly or reasonably so taken. The evaluative question presents itself to both of them as a question to which there is a right or wrong or at least a better or worse answer as to what that person should believe on this occasion.

We all face questions like this every day in deciding what to do and what to believe and in understanding the actions and beliefs of others. They are questions involving evaluation or assessment. Even in gathering

---

23. In his *Life of Alexander* Plutarch reports: "When King Darius sent him a letter asking him to accept 10,000 talents in return for the prisoners, all the land west of the river Euphrates, one of his daughters in marriage and friendship and alliance, Alexander put the terms to his companions. 'If I were Alexander,' Parmenion said, 'I would accept these terms.' 'And so would I,' said Alexander, 'if I were Parmenion.'" Quoted in Robin Lane Fox, *The Classical World*, Penguin, London, 2005, p. 229.

non-evaluative information about what is so, including the likely consequences of acting in one way rather than another, we must be sensitive
to, and make assessments of, whether one thing we believe is good reason to believe a certain other thing. Any negative metaphysical verdict
worthy of consideration cannot deny that we engage in such practices.
They involve the very thoughts and beliefs that a metaphysical investigation of the status of values in the world wants to subject to special
philosophical scrutiny. Far from denying that we have such beliefs,
metaphysical reflection must acknowledge them and account for them.
So a negative metaphysical verdict about values must accept that making
evaluative judgments is essential to intentional action and ascribing
such judgments to agents is essential to the recognition and explanation
of their acting intentionally. It cannot deny that the evaluative views we
hold are irreducible to anything purely non-evaluative, that our evaluative judgments are not always made relative to the wants or desires of
the agent or anyone else, that we treat some evaluative questions as
having right or wrong or at least better or worse answers, and that we can
reject our own or others' evaluations as wrong or unreasonable on either
evaluative or non-evaluative grounds.

It can still be thought that all this is at least, strictly speaking, consistent with a negative metaphysical verdict about values. The thought is,
to put it in terms of our original dichotomy, that everything about our
attitudes and how we act in the light of them is still on the side of the
subject or the agent or the valuer or "beholder." And all this appears to
say nothing directly about what is so independently of our taking all
those attitudes. The metaphysical verdict is not simply about our *holding*
all the evaluative opinions we do, but about *what* we hold or believe or
accept in holding those opinions.

It is tempting to put this by saying that the negative verdict accepts
that we hold the evaluative opinions we do but gives a negative answer
to the question whether we are right or correct in those opinions. But
this will not do as it stands to bring out what is at stake in the metaphysical question. Once it is conceded that our evaluative practices and
beliefs are as rich and complex and as modally sensitive as they turn out
to be, and that we can regard some of those beliefs as right and others as
wrong, it becomes more and more difficult even to formulate, let alone
defend, a general thesis about value that expresses an appropriately
metaphysical point.[24]

---

24. For a treatment of the difficulties even of formulating, let alone establishing, an
'external' verdict along these lines, see Ronald Dworkin, "Objectivity and Truth:
You'd Better Believe It," *Philosophy and Public Affairs* 1996.

To ask whether we are right or correct in holding the evaluative opinions that we do could be a way of asking whether the contents of those opinions—the things we hold or accept or believe—are right or correct or true. For instance, if we believe that an act of willful murder is vicious or evil and worthy of disapproval, then to ask whether we are right or correct in that belief is to ask whether an act of willful murder is vicious, and so on. That is an evaluative question. Most of us will answer 'Yes,' but even to answer 'No' or 'Not always' would be to offer a contrary evaluation. To give either answer, or to try to answer the question at all, is still to engage in the practice of evaluation. But the negative metaphysical verdict is not meant to be a negative answer to some evaluative question to which we give a positive answer. It cannot be an evaluative claim if, as it says, there is nothing evaluative in the world corresponding to what evaluative judgments say.

The negative metaphysical verdict is completely general; it is meant to apply to all evaluative judgments, not just those about willful murder. But even the general question whether we are *ever* right or correct in *any* of our evaluative judgments can be understood as itself an evaluative question. If we regard our evaluation of willful murder as right or correct we can say 'Yes, we are right in some (at least one) of our evaluative judgments.' That is a positive answer to the completely general question about all our evaluations on the basis of a single instance.[25] But it is not a positive answer to the question to which the metaphysical verdict is meant to give a negative answer. The metaphysical denial that anyone is ever right or correct in any evaluative judgments is not to be understood as itself an evaluative judgment.

To understand what that verdict means and implies we must therefore find some question that is left over or remains unanswered even when we have given our best answers to particular evaluative questions and so to the general evaluative question whether we are ever right in any evaluative judgments. The question (if any) that remains must be understood as a still-open question about evaluation in general. It will be a question to which the metaphysical verdict gives a negative answer, but not an evaluative answer. It is not simply a question about whether we hold certain attitudes or explain human actions in certain ways. It is

---

25. This is the way G. E. Moore answered the completely general question 'Does anyone know of the existence of things to be met with in space?' If Moore does know that here is a hand (as he obviously does), he answers that general question correctly by presenting a particular positive case. Whether Moore gives a correct or even satisfactory answer to another completely general question about human knowledge that can be expressed in those very same words is more difficult to say; it depends on what that different question is understood to be. The same appears to be so with the question of evaluation.

meant to be a question about what is so independently of anyone's making any evaluative judgments at all. But even a question expressed in those very terms can be understood as itself an evaluative question.

To ask whether our evaluative judgments are right or correct or true in the world independently of anyone's holding evaluative or other attitudes to anything could be to ask, for instance, whether an act of willful murder would be vicious or evil and worthy of disapproval independently of anyone's evaluating such an act in that or any other way. It would be the question whether in general people's holding the evaluative views they do has an effect on or is relevant to the right or correct evaluation of ways of acting. If what was said earlier about our practices is correct, and evaluative judgments are not always made relative to someone's wants or desires or other evaluative attitudes, I think the answer to this evaluative question is No. An act of willful murder could still be vicious or evil even if no one actually took that attitude toward it or toward any act of that kind. To disagree with that and insist that whether something is vicious or evil does depend on what attitudes people do or would hold toward it would be to give an opposed but still evaluative answer to the question. But the metaphysical denial of all value in the world independently of everyone's holding evaluative attitudes is not meant to be an answer to any such evaluative question.[26]

This begins to bring out the difficulty of finding a way even to formulate or express, let alone defend, an intelligible metaphysical verdict about value. This same difficulty challenged Blackburn's 'projectivist quasi-realist' account of causal beliefs and attitudes. In trying even to formulate the metaphysical question the problem was to find a form of words that does not simply either state or deny something we already express within the very way of thinking that is under metaphysical scrutiny. It was an attempt to say something about a whole way of thinking from somehow "outside" it. The problem arises again here for the same reason. To accept that we have and deploy a great many evaluative thoughts and attitudes, and that we regard some of them as right or correct or true and others as wrong or mistaken, leaves less and less room for anyone who understands and engages in those practices to find a way of saying that we are never right or correct in what we accept in any of those beliefs or attitudes.

---

26. This shows that if the acceptance of a negative metaphysical verdict about value rests on the thesis that a person's having reason to act in a certain way always depends on the wants or desires of the agent (as I claimed on p. 106 above), that thesis must be understood non-evaluatively, not as an evaluative remark about the value of something's depending on something else.

If we are never right or correct in any of our evaluative beliefs, there is a question of what the incorrectness or "error" we are said to be involved in actually amounts to. What has sometimes been called an "error" theory of value[27] says that the "error" is to be understood somehow as metaphysical, and so not simply as an evaluative "error." But that view must have some implications for an understanding of our evaluative practices as they actually are. If our being in "error" in all our evaluative judgments means that no evaluative judgments or propositions at all are true, there would be difficulty in understanding apparent evaluative disagreement. The evaluative attitudes 'Abortion is wrong' and 'No, abortion is not wrong' appear to conflict in truth-value. An "error" theory that denies truth to all evaluative judgments would imply that neither is true. It is perhaps not worth pursuing here how that could be so. Leaving aside disagreement, the falsity of all evaluative judgments might still be thought, strictly speaking, consistent with our holding all the evaluative attitudes we do. But that is not something that anyone who engages in evaluative practices and makes evaluative judgments could consistently accept. This is the same kind of inconsistency we have seen arises elsewhere.

It might seem still possible to defend a negative metaphysical verdict while insisting that there is no "error" or "mistake" involved in our evaluating things as we do. That is what Blackburn claims in the case of causation. But for any such metaphysical verdict to be intelligible and defensible in this case it must say something non-evaluative about our evaluative attitudes. It cannot be simply a remark about what those attitudes are, or about our holding the attitudes we do. It must say something about the relation between our thinking what we do and the world as it is independently of our taking those attitudes to it. It must explain or at least describe some way our evaluative attitudes fall short of or fail to capture what is so in that independent world. And it must do so in purely non-evaluative terms.

Ronald Dworkin has argued, for reasons I have just been canvassing, that there is no non-evaluative question left open or unanswered once we have made our best evaluative judgments of how things are.[28] He finds no interpretation of the words used in the attempt to express a negative metaphysical verdict about value that says anything non-evaluative that is less than preposterous. On any reading that makes sense, he finds the

---

27. Mackie, *Ethics*, p. 35, calls it that. I believe he might have been the first to use that label.

28. Dworkin, "Objectivity and Truth."

putatively metaphysical verdict to be a veiled evaluative claim. Once the 'external' or 'Archimedean' defender of a negative metaphysical verdict concedes as much as he must about the complexity of our evaluative practices and the pervasiveness of such judgments in our thought, Dworkin thinks, there is nowhere left for the theorist to stand to make a general non-evaluative negative claim about the place of value in the world.

We have seen that what is required to even express, let alone defend, any such metaphysical and so non-evaluative negative verdict about value is a metaphysically 'purified' or 'corrected' conception of what the world is really like independently of our taking evaluative attitudes toward it. I have identified what look to be obstacles to arriving at any such conception consistently with holding the beliefs and attitudes we actually have. To be in a position to assert a negative metaphysical verdict about value it is not enough to think of the world in exclusively non-evaluative terms. To declare from such a position that nothing evaluative is so in the 'purified' world one has come to accept would be to say only that nothing evaluative is said to be so by anything expressed in non-evaluative terms. That says no more than that evaluative statements are not equivalent to and do not follow from non-evaluative statements alone. That is not yet a metaphysical verdict. It is at best a logical or semantical claim about the relations among statements of two different kinds. In itself it has no metaphysical implications one way or the other.

A metaphysical thesis would be in the offing if the theorist added the further claim that the purely non-evaluative world he now has a conception of is the only world there is. That would be a way of trying to say that there are only non-evaluative facts; that evaluative judgments or propositions state nothing that is so. But there would remain the question of how that is to be understood. If it implies that only non-evaluative propositions are true, it looks as if we would be left with the idea that all our evaluative judgments are false after all. That is not something we could accept consistently with holding evaluative attitudes ourselves and making sense of our own and others' beliefs and intentional actions in the ways we do.

Allan Gibbard agrees that we treat evaluative or what he calls normative[29] questions of what to do as 'fact-like' questions. Accepting evaluative or normative judgments in answer to such questions, and "reasoning . . . as

---

29. I think nothing relevant to the discussion here turns on whether we call the judgments in question 'normative' or 'evaluative.' Even if those labels carry different implications in some contexts, what is in question here is the relation between judgments of either kind and judgments that are neither normative nor evaluative.

if there are such facts of what to do," he thinks, "is not to commit an error."[30] He thinks we regard normative questions as capable of right or wrong answers, that we are right to do so, and even that the answers can be "true or false, independent of our accepting them."[31] Given our engagement in our normative practices as they are, he thinks we cannot "deny that in some important senses, normative knowledge can be had."[32]

Gibbard accepts all this as true of our evaluative concepts and practices, but he is not content to take "unexplained normative facts" as "brute features" of the world.[33] He thinks more can be done to explain the special features of normative thought, even without seeking to analyze or reduce normative or evaluative notions into equivalent but non-normative terms, and without denying that there are normative facts.

> We can explain belief in them ... without helping ourselves to normative facts at the outset, to facts of what's good or bad, or to facts of what is the thing to do.[34]

When we think that a particular action a ought to be done, for instance, or that there is more reason to do something b than not to do it, that thought can be said to be true or false on a "minimalist" conception of truth according to which to claim that it is true that p is just to claim that p. If every true thought can be said to express a fact, and we accept, and so accept as true, that a ought to be done, or that there is more reason to do b than not to do it, then on this view we accept that there are normative facts; there are true normative thoughts.

But these facts, thoughts, and beliefs, according to Gibbard, "are built from concepts: property concepts and relation concepts, among others.[35] Our normative thoughts have certain distinctive features because they are built from normative concepts, but there is no need to assume anything normative or evaluative in order to explain those special features. States of affairs, on the other hand, "are built from properties, relations, and the like," not from concepts or ways of thinking, and we do not have to appeal to normative properties or relations or states of affairs to explain our normative thinking. In fact, for Gibbard, "there is no such thing as a specially normative state of affairs; all states of affairs are natural."[36]

---

30. Gibbard, *Thinking How to Live*, Harvard University Press, Cambridge, Mass., 2003, p. 37.

31. Ibid., p. 183.

32. Ibid., p. 184.

33. Ibid., pp. 191, 184.

34. Ibid., p. 183.

35. Ibid., p. 181.

36. Ibid., p.181.

This does not mean only that all states of affairs that hold in the natural world are natural. It makes the stronger and explicitly metaphysical claim that natural states of affairs are the only states of affairs there are. This also means that there are "no peculiarly normative, non-natural properties."[37] Nothing in the world has the *property* of being what ought to be done, for instance, or being something there is more reason to do than not do. Nothing anywhere has any such property. So even though our distinctively normative thoughts and beliefs can be said to be true and to express normative or evaluative facts, we never truly ascribe a normative property to anything or truly assert that some normative or evaluative states of affairs hold.

This is meant to be a negative verdict of some kind about values or the normative. It is a denial of something, but it is not to be understood as denying anything normative or evaluative. There is a way of taking the claim that nothing has the *property* of being what ought to be done that would make it a normative or evaluative judgment. If there can be a "minimalist" understanding of the attribution of a property to something, analogous to "minimalism" about the attribution of truth to something, then to say that a has the property F would just be to say that a is F. On that view, to say that there is nothing that has the property of being what ought to be done would be to say that there is nothing that ought to be done. That implies, for instance, that if there is a struggling, panicking child in a swimming pool, giving help to the child is not something that ought to be done. That would be a normative or evaluative judgment.

That is not how Gibbard's denial is to be understood. His claim that nothing has any normative or evaluative *properties* is not to be domesticated by that "minimalist" strategy into what would then be a normative judgment. His denial is meant to carry substantial metaphysical weight as a verdict about the domain of the normative in general. It is "external" to normative thinking: a "commentary on normative thinking, concepts, and their truth-makers that [isn't] part of normative thinking itself or equivalent to it."[38] There remains a question of what exactly that non-evaluative "external" verdict says, and what it implies about the normative facts we all believe in. If it says only that there are no normative facts in the world of exclusively naturalistic properties, relations, and states of affairs, it would say no more than that there are no normative facts in the natural world: that normative facts are different from naturalistic facts and are not implied by them. A stronger metaphysical denial would say

---

37. Ibid., p. 192.
38. Ibid., p. 186.

that the world of natural properties, relations, and states of affairs is the only world there is. But Gibbard finds that he cannot reach a position from which to pronounce such a satisfyingly general non-normative verdict on the whole domain of the normative all at once.

For Gibbard the metaphysical difference between naturalistic and normative facts is to be established by showing that

> To explain belief in natural fact adequately, we must assume a natural world of which we are a part. We must start with a realm of naturalistic facts. To explain belief in normative facts, in contrast, we need not start with a realm of normative facts.[39]

This appears to offer the prospect of a certain kind of unmasking explanation of normative facts in general. If no normative or evaluative facts are needed to explain how we come to believe in them, but naturalistic facts are needed to explain why we come to believe in the natural world, the natural world could be said to be the only world there is in the sense that it is the only world we need to appeal to to explain all our normative and non-normative beliefs about it.

Complete success of a metaphysical program along these lines would require both that all beliefs in normative facts be explained by naturalistic facts alone and also, equally important, that all beliefs in naturalistic facts be explained without assuming any normative facts or any unexplained normative or evaluative beliefs. It is doubtful that either requirement can be met, for reasons Gibbard tries to take account of. The explanation would start with facts of the natural world, including the presence of people who have beliefs about the natural world and are also faced with questions about what to do. Rather than taking their pondering and deciding what to do as their seeking or accepting normative or evaluative beliefs about what ought to be done—the very thing to be explained—Gibbard starts with something he regards as more fundamental, and so more explanatory: "weighing factors for or against various courses of action in various contingencies."[40] That is a psychological state that he thinks is "naturalistically recognizable."[41] That presumably means it can be found to be present among human beings using only concepts that pick out aspects of the exclusively natural world. "Weighing" as Gibbard understands it is "calculating what to do on a certain pattern, a pattern we could program a robot to mimic."[42]

---

39. Ibid., p. 183.
40. Ibid., p. 189.
41. Ibid., p. 195.
42. Ibid., p. 190.

If this "weighing" or planning or considering what to do is recogniz-able as part of the natural world it is presumably recognizable on the basis of the actions agents can be observed to perform because of being in such a state. But there is a question whether such actions and states could be recognized and understood using only concepts applicable to the exclusively natural world. "Weighing" what to do cannot be simply a matter of a person's being the site or repository of the operation of certain factors or forces that eventually determine his movements in the way the various forces operating on a passenger in a roller-coaster determine the way he moves. For the "weighing" to be relevant to a person's acting intentionally, it seems that it must involve the agent's thinking of his actions and their consequences in certain determinate ways and accept-ing some considerations and not others as counting in favor of doing one thing rather than another. This means that the agent must be capable of certain kinds of thoughts and intentional attitudes the descriptions of which capture the particular ways he thinks or feels about what is so and about his acting in a certain way. Substituting co-extensive terms within the description of the attitudes relevant to the agent's acting as he does will not necessarily preserve the truth of the ascription.

If agents' thinking and assessing things in those determinate ways is part of what Gibbard thinks of as the natural world, it looks as if holding normative or evaluative beliefs about what ought to be done or what there is good reason to do would also be part of the natural world. That would presumably mean that the normative contents of those beliefs cannot be expressed in exclusively naturalistic terms; if they could, they would have lost their normative force. But Gibbard seeks a form of "expressiv-ist" explanation of the normative that would "obviate the need for natu-ralistic mumbo-jumbo" even in the contents of agents' beliefs.[43] The expressivist strategy is to start with states of mind that are not described in terms of their contents as beliefs at all, and eventually to "identify" such states with the holding of normative beliefs. But the states of mind from which such an explanation would start involve the person's thinking and meaning and understanding things in one way rather than others, and this Gibbard sees as an obstacle to the full realization of a satisfyingly general negative verdict on the domain of the normative as a whole.

The threat he sees lies in something he expresses as "meaning is nor-mative" or "the concept of what a term means is itself a normative con-cept."[44] The threat seems real, given Gibbard's conception of what is and what is not part of the exclusively natural world. A person's saying

---

43. Ibid.
44. Ibid., p. 191.

something and meaning it in a certain way, or thinking of things in a certain determinate way rather than others, does seem to involve the person's taking something as reason to say or accept one thing and not another. It involves some recognition of what is required for meaning or thinking something in a determinate way and a capacity to intentionally do what conforms to those standards. None of this need take the form of explicitly rehearsed thoughts in the person's mind at the time of action or expression, or at any other time. But a person's meaning or thinking something in a determinate way on a particular occasion would not be intelligible without the ascription of such capacities to the person.

Gibbard rejects any strictly naturalistic understanding of "states of affairs in which thoughts and meanings figure."[45] But thoughts and meanings figure in the "weighing" or planning attitudes from which a potentially unmasking metaphysical explanation of all normative or evaluative beliefs is supposed to begin. This is further reason to adopt what Gibbard calls the "oblique analysis" favored by expressivists: to "elucidate the concepts of ought, meaning, and mental content by saying what it is to *judge* or *believe* that a person ought to do something, or that he means such-and-such or that he is thinking that such-and-such."[46] A "naturalistic expressivist" who takes agents' thinking and meaning things to be part of the fully natural world could perhaps "elucidate" the concept of what ought to be done or what there is reason to do in this "oblique" way. It would not exactly provide a naturalistic *explanation* of people's holding the evaluative beliefs they do, but it would put the "naturalistic expressivist" in a position to announce that the natural world is the only world there is, or that "the basic fabric of the world is naturalistic."[47] The natural world contains thinkers with evaluative attitudes, and that is all that is needed to explain their thinking and doing all the things they do.

But Gibbard rightly takes the domain of the normative to extend even into matters of meaning and thinking, so the judgings or believings or other attitudes thought to be unproblematically available to the "naturalistic expressivist" for his "elucidation" of the normative can no longer be taken for granted. A more sophisticated "expressivist" account is called for.

The most that either kind of expressivist can do is to say what is involved in someone's *accepting* that *a* ought to be done or that *b* is reason to do *x*. For Gibbard the "psychic state" of accepting such a claim is a state of planning to act in a certain way. But Gibbard's more

---

45. Ibid., p. 191.
46. Ibid., p. 193.
47. Ibid., p. 194.

sophisticated expressivist sees that psychic state of planning as the person's meaning or thinking of things in certain ways, which in itself involves the use of normative concepts. Those normative concepts are therefore to be elucidated by finding the psychic state that is involved in *accepting* something of the form '____ means . . . ' or '____ thinks . . . ' This would bring to the surface yet another normative claim still to be elucidated by that same kind of expressivist treatment, and that claim in turn would yield yet another normative claim to be acknowledged, and so on forever. For every expressivist elucidation of someone's employment of a normative concept, there would be yet another state involving the use of just such a concept still to be elucidated. "This regress never strikes non-normative bedrock," Gibbard says.[48]

This "regress-style expressivism" leaves us with no satisfactory explanation in exclusively naturalistic, non-normative terms of the whole domain of the normative in general all at once. Gibbard concedes that it "fails to constitute an independent metanormative position."[49] If the regress never reaches "non-normative bedrock," this means that expressivism also does not explain in what it regards as exclusively naturalistic terms even how we come to have non-normative *naturalistic* beliefs about the world. Our having such beliefs also involves our meaning and thinking things in certain ways, and taking one thing to be reason to believe another. If we do not completely escape reliance on the normative even in elucidating the concepts involved in holding non-normative, naturalistic beliefs, we never reach an "independent metanormative position" in understanding our possession of any concepts and beliefs at all.

We saw that the "naturalistic expressivist" who treats meaning and determinate thinking as part of the exclusively natural world would be in a "metanormative" position to declare that "the basic fabric of the world is naturalistic." He would have appealed to nothing beyond what he takes to be naturalistic truths to account for or at least to elucidate normative beliefs. But, as Gibbard explains, "the regress-style expressivist" cannot say that only naturalistic facts have been appealed to: "by this test for what the basic fabric of the world includes, *oughts* and naturalistic *iss* qualify equally."[50]

I think Gibbard is right to insist that "we cannot do without normative concepts"[51] in explaining how we have come to have all the normative

---

48. Ibid., p. 194.
49. Ibid., p. 187. This is Dworkin's charge against all would-be "external" non-normative views. See pp. 116–117 above.
50. Ibid., p. 194.
51. Ibid., p. 196.

and even all the non-normative concepts and beliefs we know we have. This means we have not reached a satisfactory non-normative or meta-normative explanation or verdict about the domain of the normative in general. We have not reached a position from which we can consistently accept a negative metaphysical verdict about value or the normative. This perhaps reveals in yet another way the difficulty of doing full justice to the ways we actually think of the world while at the same time accepting a negative verdict about the relation between what we think in those ways of thinking and the fully independent world we all believe in.

Our failure to reach and sustain a negative metaphysical verdict about values in any of these ways does not amount to a proof that it is impossible, of course. But again the conclusion seems to me inescapable. Attending to our evaluative judgments and practices as they actually are leaves us unable to see them all together from a position that somehow reveals their relation to an independent world in which none of them hold. The combination of the irreducibility, the indispensability, and the pervasiveness of evaluative judgments defeats the attempt to reach a completely general negative metaphysical verdict about them. What I find most remarkable about this recognizable failure is how little effect it seems to have on the apparently unshakeable conviction that a negative metaphysical verdict about values in the independent world simply must be right.

5

Indispensability

So far we have found no consistent way of reaching a satisfying meta-physical verdict about the kinds of judgments involved in the three fundamental areas of our thought that we have considered. At best we are left with no metaphysically satisfying understanding of our beliefs about causal dependence, necessity, or value in relation to the independent world we thereby think about. Trying to get a better understanding of the source of the obstacles we have encountered might lead to a firmer sense of what we are really after in pursuing the metaphysical urge and of whether and how the obstacles can be avoided or overcome.

A reassuringly positive verdict would have been reached if it could have been shown that the very contents of the things we believe in the areas in question can be reduced without remainder to something that is uncontroversially so in the world as it is independently of us and our responses to it. But no such straightforward reduction seemed plausible in any case. A satisfying negative metaphysical verdict appears unreachable if those beliefs are irreducible in that way and we cannot avoid thinking in causal, modal, and evaluative terms in the very attempt to accept the verdict that they do not really capture anything that is so in the independent world. Accepting such a negative verdict is inconsistent with accepting all the things we have to accept in order to reach it. But because of their indispensability there appears to be no option of simply abandoning those ways of thinking and accepting a negative metaphysical verdict that would undermine them. They cannot be abandoned if we are to think about the world at all.

Without suggesting that we have found anything approaching a demonstrative proof of the indispensability of those ways of thinking, I believe a strong case can be made for it. It is difficult to deny that belief in causal or counterfactual conditional dependence is essential to thought of a world of objects that behave as they do independently of us and our responses. Accepting that some things hold necessarily is needed for acknowledging the validity of an inference from one proposition to another with no possibility of going from truth to falsity. Intentional actions, including the acceptance of one belief on the basis of others, involve irreducibly evaluative attitudes. We can believe certain things, and intentionally act in one way rather than another, only because we take something as reason to believe or act as we do. It is difficult to see how anyone could think of a world and think of himself as a thinker and an agent in that world without holding some such attitudes. Whatever we do, we remain immersed in or committed to all those irreducible ways of thinking.

The indispensability of certain ways of thinking is central to meta-physics of a broadly Kantian variety. But even if we grant the indispens-ability of the ways of thinking we have considered, what metaphysical conclusions can be drawn from it? For Kant indispensability was the key to the very possibility of putting metaphysics once and for all on the secure path of a science. I want to suggest to the contrary that the indispens-ability of those irreducible ways of thinking represents an insurmountable obstacle to the kind of metaphysical satisfaction I think we seek.

What is perhaps the most compelling application of the idea of indis-pensability appears in philosophy long before Kant. Descartes drew attention to a particular instance of it as the starting-point of his meta-physics. He was suspicious or uncertain of much that he had been taught or thought he had learned, and wanting to get back to the very beginning and start from the ground up, he concentrated on his own thinking. He found it was something he could not get below, or behind, or bring into doubt. He saw that his thought 'Cogito' or 'I think' must be true each time he thinks or pronounces it. He could not possibly deny the truth of that very thought and be right. To deny it would be to say or think that it is not true. But thinking that he does not think would still be a case of thinking, so his original thought that he thinks would be true after all.

Descartes eventually drew many rich epistemological and meta-physical conclusions from this starting-point. For our purposes what is of most interest is the special character of that starting-point itself. The fact that the proposition 'I think' cannot be truly denied by the thinker of it gives it a very special status. Descartes says that his 'I think' is "necessarily true whenever it is put forward by me or conceived in my mind."[1] We can see why he says this, but it cannot mean that it is necessarily true that he thinks in the sense that it could not possibly have been false that he thinks. There are possible circumstances under which Descartes does not think; some of them are now actual. Descartes was thinking in 1638, but he thinks no more. So what was true once, and was then known by him—that he thinks—is no longer true. But still, necessarily, whenever Descartes thought he was thinking, he was. He could not possibly have been right in denying it.

So the fact that Descartes thinks, or the fact that I think, or the fact that anyone thinks, are all things that can fail, or could have failed, to hold. In Descartes's case, what was once so—that he thinks—fails to hold right now. In my case, it is true now that I think, but it could have failed to be true even now, and in a few years it will be true no longer. All such facts of people thinking are contingent in the sense that things could have been (and, as we know, actually will be) otherwise, but they are contingent facts with a very special status. 'I think' could not fail to hold while it is being thought to be true by the thinker who is its subject. Necessarily, whenever anyone thinks 'I think,' it is true. And it also must be true if the thinker is thinking anything else.

Since 'I think' has this special undeniable status for each thinker, anything else that must be true if that thinker thinks must also have this same undeniable status for that thinker. The original security and distinctive invulnerability of 'I think' will extend outward to every other proposition that must be true if 'I think' is true. This was the basis of Descartes's metaphysical strategy. He saw first that what is true of 'I think' must also be true of 'I am, I exist.' That is because, necessarily, if I think then I exist; I could not possibly fail to exist if I think. So my existence must have the same special or distinctively invulnerable status for me as my thinking does.

This does not mean that I can see that I enjoy (if that is the right word) necessary existence—that I could not possibly fail to exist. Rather, as it is with my thinking, so it is with my existing; there was a time when I did not exist, and there will be a time when I exist no more. So 'I exist' has not been found to be necessarily true in the sense that it could not possibly have been false. But, necessarily, it is true that I exist whenever I pronounce or think 'I exist,' or even whenever I deny it. I could not deny it and be right, since to deny it I must think, and if I think I must exist.

---

1. R. Descartes, *The Philosophical Writings of Descartes* (tr. John Cottingham, Robert Stoothoff, Dugald Murdoch), Cambridge University Press, Cambridge, 1985, vol. 2, p. 17. Descartes actually says this of the proposition 'I am, I exist,' not of 'I think.' But both have the same undeniable status.

Like 'I exist,' everything else that is a necessary condition of the truth of 'I think' for a given thinker must also be true if he thinks. If there are any interesting further conditions of this kind, then none of them, whatever they might be, could be correctly denied by that thinker. It is simply not possible for a person to be right in denying the truth of anything that is a necessary condition of that person's thinking. So if there are some necessary conditions of a thinker's thinking, even if they themselves express something that holds only contingently and could have been false under some circumstances, they will belong to a very special class of propositions for that thinker. The thinker could not possibly deny them and be right.

This idea was richly exploited by Kant. He was interested not just in the thinking of an individual thinker, but in the possibility of thinking in general by anyone. And since he regarded even *experience* of a world as impossible without thought, he focused on the necessary conditions of any possible thought or experience. The overall project of his *Critique of Pure Reason* was to establish that there are certain concepts or ways of thinking that are necessary for thinking or experiencing anything at all. If such ways of thinking could be identified and their distinctive status established, it was then to be shown that any world we could experience and think about must be as those ways of thinking say it is. That would be a firm, positive metaphysical verdict about those ways of thinking. There would be no possibility of our correctly finding things to be otherwise. For Kant this was the only way metaphysics could be a legitimate intellectual enterprise with the possibility of secure results. As long as anyone thinks or experiences anything at all, the necessary conditions of any thought or experience would be guaranteed to be fulfilled in the world the person thereby thinks about or experiences.

Since for Kant those ways of thinking that are necessary for any thinking at all express necessary features of any world, he thought the reflection that leads to those results must be a priori, completely independent of all possible sense experience. That is because he took necessity to be a "sure criterion" or a "secure indication" of the a priori; "if we have a proposition which in being thought is thought as *necessary*," he says, "it is an *a priori* judgment."[2] But Kant was optimistic about the prospects of this a priori kind of metaphysics because, as he put it, its "subject-matter is not the nature of things, which is inexhaustible, but

---

2. Kant, *Critique of Pure Reason* (tr. N. Kemp Smith), Macmillan, London, 1953, B3, p. 43. Further implications of this assumption are discussed in ch. 3 above.

the understanding which passes judgment upon the nature of things."
And since "these *a priori* possessions of the understanding . . . have not
to be sought for without [or, as he put it elsewhere, "there is no need to
go far afield, since I come upon them in my own self"],[3] [they] cannot
remain hidden from us, and in all probability are sufficiently small in
extent to allow of our apprehending them in their completeness."[4]

Despite Kant's insistence that we can come to know of these necessary
conditions only by a priori means, the distinctive invulnerability of his
metaphysical results does not turn primarily on our having pure a priori
insight into them. Pure reflection independently of all experience is not
in itself infallible; reaching a conclusion by purely a priori means is no
guarantee that we must be right. The special and specially invulnerable
character of Kant's metaphysical results comes from the indispensability
of the propositions in question for the possibility of any thought or
experience. The *necessity* is what is crucial. If none of those propositions could possibly be false if anything is even so much as thought to be
true, then no attempt to deny or even cast doubt on any of them could be
right. If we knew that Kant's conclusions about the indispensability of
those propositions are correct, we would know that no thinking could
correctly lead us to reject any of those propositions and think of the
world in other ways incompatible with them. Belief in anything that has
that distinctively invulnerable status would be secure whether the
invulnerability had been discovered by a priori insight into something
or in some other way. What matters is the special status of the propositions in question, not how we come to know of it.

That is not to say that it is easy to show, of certain propositions, that
they occupy this special indispensable position in our thought. Some
propositions that all thinkers accept have a certain special status simply
in being necessarily true; they could not possibly be false under any
circumstances. No one could possibly be right in denying something
that is necessarily true. But the Kantian metaphysical project was not
primarily concerned with propositions that are necessarily true and
cannot be denied without contradiction. All such propositions are what
Kant called 'analytic': they reveal only which concepts are 'contained'
in which other concepts. That yields only conditional truths about the
way things must be *if* they are also a certain other way. Kant sought
categorical or non-conditional metaphysical conclusions about the way
the world is, or the way things are. They would be non-'analytic,' or

---

3. Ibid., Axiv, p. 10.
4. Ibid., A13 = B26, pp. 59–60.

'synthetic,' propositions that are invulnerable or undeniable because they express necessary conditions of thought and experience in general.

The truths Kant sought could even be said to be about the way the world *must* be, but not simply what could not possibly have been otherwise. The metaphysical conclusions were to be arrived at by discovering how things must be or what must be so *if* anything is thought or experienced at all. Such a conditional statement is itself a claim of necessity, but it could be true even if the necessity it speaks of holds between things that are in themselves contingent and could have been otherwise. That there is any thought and experience at all is, it seems, a contingent fact; there could have been no such thing. What must be so if there is any thought or experience can therefore also be something that in that same way could have been otherwise. Within the Kantian enterprise, what is said to be necessary is not simply that there is such a thing as thought and experience, or that any of the substantive conclusions about the world that can be shown to follow from that are true.[5] The necessity resides in the connection between the two; in the impossibility of any of those substantive conclusions' being false, given the not-truly-deniable but still contingent starting-point that there is thought and experience.

For our purposes here it is enough to appreciate the general structure of this ambitious project and to get some sense of what it can promise. If Kant's 'deductions' of those necessary conditions as he understands them were successful, they would yield substantial general conclusions about the world. It would have been shown, for instance, that there are enduring objects in space and time, that all events stand in causal relations to other events that happen, that there are thinking, experiencing, active subjects who hold just these and other such general beliefs about the world. If Kant is right, all these things must be so if anyone thinks or has experiences of anything at all; they are among the necessary conditions of all thought and experience. They state the way things must be, given that there is any thought and experience.

If we give to those propositions that have that special role in our thought the names 'P,' 'Q,' 'R,' and so on, the abstract form of Kant's results can be expressed as: necessarily, if there is any thought or experience at all, P and Q and R and so on are true. Even if that is correct, and the propositions P, Q, R, and all the other indispensable propositions have that distinctive status in our thought, we might nonetheless still be able to think of what it would be like for some or all of them not to be true. It would be for there to be no enduring objects in space, for

---

5. Kant is not always sound on this point. He sometimes speaks without qualification of the synthetic *a priori* results of his investigation as themselves 'necessary.'

instance, or no causal connections between things, or no thinking subjects, and so on. There appears, at least at first sight, to be no contradiction or impossibility involved in our conceiving of things' having been that way. In that sense, we can make sense of and concede that P and Q and R and so on *could* themselves have been false. But what we cannot conceive if Kant is right—what is not possible—is for statements with the special status of P and Q and R and so on to be false if anyone thinks or experiences anything. So in conceiving of circumstances in which they would be false (if we can), we must be conceiving of circumstances in which there would be no thought or experience either. But surely that is something we can conceive of. Not only is it possible in that sense for there to have been no thought or experience; I think there was a time when there actually was no thought or experience.

Just as no one could possibly be right in thinking, of himself, 'I do not think,' so the special status of the propositions P and Q and R and so on means that no one could ever be right in thinking that any of those propositions are false. To deny even one of those propositions would be enough to guarantee that all of them are true. So anyone who arrived at a metaphysical view of the world that conflicts with the truth of one or another of P or Q or R and so on would have to be wrong if those propositions have that distinctive position in our thought. The truth of what that person denies would be a necessary condition of anyone's thinking or experiencing anything. So he could not deny it and be right.

It would be no help to try to add in a conciliatory spirit that of course we cannot help *believing* that P and Q and R and so on are true, that for perfectly understandable reasons we cannot avoid engaging in the "fiction" that they are all true, but that they are not really true in the world after all. No such denial of anything in the distinctive class could be right, if there is such a class of indispensable propositions. The kind of invulnerability Descartes correctly claimed for his 'I think' and 'I exist' would extend to everything that is a necessary condition of anyone's thinking anything at all. The success of a project along these lines would give us a unique set of assured results and a method for showing that anyone who would deny any of them must be wrong.

The absolute security of this kind of Kantian position might be enough in itself to raise doubts about how or whether such strong conclusions could ever be reached. The propositions we are calling P, Q, R, and so on are meant to state what are necessary conditions of any thought or experience at all. They are statements about how things are, but they are not guaranteed to be true simply by being in themselves necessarily true. They are statements about a world that we can think of as being the way it is whether it is thought to be that way or not, or even whether anyone thinks or experiences anything at all. Most of those propositions themselves say or imply nothing about anyone's thinking or experiencing anything. But propositions that have that special status are to be discovered by inferring or 'deducing' them from nothing more than the possibility of anyone's thinking or experiencing anything. That is the Kantian strategy.

This is what makes the metaphysical project look both so exciting and at the same time so questionable. Can we proceed by secure necessary steps from our thinking and experiencing things in certain ways, or even from our thinking and experiencing anything at all, to conclusions about how things actually are whether they are thought about or experienced or not? Can you get a whole independent world out of nothing more than thought of a world or a world-like course of experience? Can you get a rabbit out of an empty silk hat? Many philosophers since Kant have argued that no positive metaphysical results are possible along these lines.

You do not have to deny the very possibility of metaphysics to recognize two obvious sources of difficulty for this Kantian program. Everything begins for Kant with the conditions of thinking something. Any thought or experience must be *of* or *about* something, so no one could have thought or experience of anything at all without some concepts in terms of which to make sense of it. He accordingly focuses on the necessary conditions of *possessing* and *deploying* certain concepts, not simply on the conditional necessity with which one concept must apply to something if a certain other concept applies to it. Concepts for Kant are "predicates of possible judgements,"[6] so in order to think or experience anything one must be capable of judgment—of thinking that such-and-such is so. That in turn requires a capacity to think of things' being so or not so independently of the thinking of it. And that requires making sense of a distinction between a thinking subject with his or her thoughts and experiences on the one hand and something or other that is independent of a thinking subject on the other—the truth or falsity of what the thinker thinks or experiences to be so.

It is out of the need to make sense of and deploy some such fundamental distinction between a person's thoughts and what those thoughts are about that Kant eventually derives the need for a conception of a rich world of enduring objects in space and time containing events in law-like relations of cause and effect to one another, with thinking, experiencing subjects who believe and act for reasons that other agents can make sense of in interacting with them as they do. The richest results in Kant's philosophy are to be found within the details of these demonstrations of the indispensability of such very general ways of thinking.

---

6. Kant, *Critique of Pure Reason*, A69 = B94, p. 106.

These conditions as understood so far are requirements on *thought;* we must be capable of thinking in certain ways or making certain kinds of judgments in order to think or experience anything at all. We must *think* there is a world of enduring, causally interacting objects, for instance. Or, generalizing to all the allegedly distinctive propositions P and Q and R and so on, this first step of the Kantian strategy is of the form:

(1) Necessarily, if there is any thought and experience at all then thinkers think that P is true, think that Q is true, think that R is true, and so on.

This obviously is not something it would be easy to establish. The more determinate the contents of the propositions P and Q and R and so on are thought to be, the more difficult it would be to show that just those very thoughts are needed for any thought and experience at all, or that those very propositions must be included in any possible thinker's conception of a world. This first step involves a strong claim of absolute indispensability of certain determinate ways of thinking, and it would take strong argument to prove it. That is the first kind of difficulty confronting the Kantian strategy.

But even a completely successful demonstration at that first step would yield only a conclusion about the indispensability of certain ingredients in anyone's *conception* of the world. It would say that we have to think of the world in certain determinate ways in order to think of it at all. Every thinker must accept P and Q and R and so on, but that in itself does not imply that any of those propositions do or must hold in the world. That would require a second step, to a conclusion not just about how thinkers think or even must think things are, but a stronger conclusion about how things are. That is the kind of metaphysical result Kant wants to reach. It would be a metaphysical conclusion about what the world all thinkers think about is like, and it is to be reached by reflection on the necessary conditions of anyone's thinking anything at all.

Reaching such a conclusion from what I have called the first step of Kant's reasoning would require a step from how all thinkers do or must think of the world to a conclusion about how the world is. It would be a step from facts about thinkers and their thoughts to facts of the world that in general carry no implications about thinkers thinking anything. It would lead to a conclusion of the form:

(2) Necessarily, if there is any thought and experience at all then P and Q and R and so on are true.

This represents the full Kantian position described earlier. It says not only that P and Q and R and so on must be accepted by any thinker, and so included in any thinker's conception of the world. It says that P and Q and R and so on must be true in any world that anyone thinks about. That is why no one could deny any of them and be right.

Reaching this conclusion presents the second obvious difficulty for the prospects of Kantian metaphysics. The first question was how the weaker claim (1) is to be established. Now the question is how it is possible to move with some assurance of correctness from (1) to the stronger claim (2). If it is established that thinkers must think of the world in certain ways, can we infer that the world must be the ways those thinkers think it is? It is not true in general that if someone thinks something is true then what he thinks is true. Even if there is something that everyone thinks, it does not follow that it is true. Nor does the truth of something follow from the fact that everyone has to think it, or cannot avoid thinking that it is true. How, then, can the stronger Kantian conclusions about what the world is like be reached by necessary steps from weaker claims about how people must think the world is? This is a huge, complicated problem. It is the more serious of the two obstacles to secure metaphysical conclusions about the world as Kant understands them.

Kant's way of overcoming this second obstacle was idealism. The idea is that the world must be as we must unavoidably think and experience it to be. That for Kant is the only explanation of how we can have a priori knowledge of the necessary structure of the world by this reflective means. The world of which we have such a priori knowledge must conform to the necessary conditions of our thinking about it or experiencing it. The world of which we can know a priori that propositions with the special status of P and Q and R and so on are true is a world that must conform in general to "our" necessary ways of thinking of and experiencing it; it is in that sense "our" world. Such a world could not deviate, in general, from the ways we think (and must think) of it. That is why the ways of thinking required for any thought or experience must also be true of the world we thereby think about and experience.

This is idealism. But it is a very special kind of idealism: what Kant calls "transcendental idealism." "I entitle *transcendental*," he says, "all knowledge which is occupied not so much with objects as with . . . our knowledge of objects in so far as this . . . knowledge is possible a priori."[7] Since all knowledge of necessities is gained a priori, knowledge of the necessary conditions of thought and experience must be gained a priori. If those conditions express substantial truths about the world, to ask

---

7. Ibid., B25, p. 59.

how knowledge of the world is possible by this means is to ask how that knowledge is possible in so far as it is a priori. So the answer will be part of 'transcendental' philosophy. And the answer is that we can get such a priori knowledge of the world only because the world of which we get it is a world that cannot fail to conform to the general conditions of our thought about it. That is a form of idealism. But since it is the only explanation of how we can get a priori knowledge of the world, it is idealism invoked on "transcendental" grounds. Thus, "transcendental idealism."

I will not pause long over this way of overcoming the second obstacle. Transcendental idealism can seem too high a price to pay for the prospect of metaphysical satisfaction. One can even wonder what we would get if we were willing to pay that price. The world transcendental idealism would guarantee us metaphysical knowledge of is a world that must be in general just as thinkers must think it is. But is there a world like that? Could there be? And even if there could, is the world we live in actually like that? How could such a thing be discovered to be so, or not so? It is not something we could conclude directly from the fact that we think of the world in certain ways. Nor could we conclude it from the fact that we *must* think of the world in certain ways. That would be to draw a conclusion about what the world is like from facts about how thinkers must think the world is. But that is just the transition from the first to the second and more problematic step of the Kantian strategy. It is a step across the kind of gap that transcendental idealism is meant to bridge or obliterate. If we acknowledge the possibility of such a gap at all, transcendental idealism would leave us with the very doubts about the Kantian enterprise that it was supposed to overcome.

Acknowledging a difference in general between our believing something and its being so is not to deny or doubt that the world is in fact as we must believe it to be. To have beliefs about the world at all is to hold those beliefs to be true. And if there are some beliefs we *must* hold about the world if we think at all, then in those respects we do believe that the world is in fact as we must believe it to be. But that offers no metaphysical reassurance about the relation between our beliefs and the world independent of them. The metaphysical question is not simply about what we believe about the world, or even what we must believe about it. It is a further question about the extent to which, or the respects in which, the independent world matches up to all the beliefs we hold about it, including beliefs we cannot help holding. That metaphysical question is still open when we have reached only the first of the two steps of the Kantian enterprise. The second and stronger step is what is meant to take us beyond that to a metaphysically satisfying answer.

I think trying to reach even the first Kantian step, by reflecting on necessary connections only among the ways we think of the world, promises important metaphysical benefits of its own. Even without reaching metaphysical conclusions about the way things are, an exploration of the necessary connections among fundamental ways of thinking can be expected to reveal certain limits or obstacles to the richer kind of metaphysical satisfaction I think we seek. Recognizing such constraints on what metaphysical reflection could possibly provide, and understanding the source of those constraints, could itself offer a certain kind of philosophical illumination. It might even be called a 'metaphysical' outcome, but not in the form of a conclusion about what the independent world is really like. This is an idea I will try to explain.

P. F. Strawson in his *Individuals, The Bounds of Sense*, and other works has pursued to impressive lengths an effort to reach the first step of the basically Kantian enterprise. It is a matter of tracing out the intricate connections among the conditions required for any thought and experience of an objective world at all. Like Kant, Strawson too focused on predication and the possibility of judgment. He was never tempted by what he saw as the excesses of transcendental idealism. And he came to acknowledge the difficulty of moving, without the help of idealism, from a weaker claim about how we do or must think of the world to a stronger claim about how things are.[8] He drew back from that dubious step. He saw his hard-won claims of necessity as taking us no further than connections between ways of thinking: what he calls "conceptual connections"[9] or "a certain sort of interdependence of conceptual capacities and beliefs."[10] He thought tracing out these relations of interdependence can reveal "connections between the major structural features or elements of our conceptual scheme,"[11] but not necessarily any further connections between that scheme and the world itself that we think about. This is to concede the impossibility of reaching positive metaphysical conclusions about the world directly from the necessary conditions of thought and experience. It is to remain at the first of the two steps of Kantian metaphysical reflection, where only the conditions of belief or acceptance are at stake, not the truth of what is thereby believed or accepted.

---

8. See P. F. Strawson, *Skepticism and Naturalism: Some Varieties*, Methuen, London, 1985, ch. 1.

9. Ibid., p. 23.

10. Ibid., p. 21.

11. Ibid., p. 23.

That first and weaker step says of certain propositions P and Q and R and so on that, necessarily, if there is any thought and experience at all then thinkers think those propositions are true. This does not imply that any of those propositions are true. Only the second of the two Kantian steps claims truth for those distinctive propositions. But even the weaker thesis implies that no thinker could consistently deny any proposition that occupies this special indispensable position in our thought. Anyone who denied any of those propositions would also accept them, since denying them involves thinking, and accepting them is required for thought.

This means that if there is a class of propositions whose acceptance is indispensable to thought, anyone who denies any of those propositions will be inconsistent in believing what she believes. The second and stronger step of the Kantian reasoning implies that anyone who denies any of those indispensable propositions will be wrong in denying them. Denying them involves thinking, and their truth is required for thought. This would mean that no metaphysical denial of any of the propositions P or Q or R and so on could possibly be correct. To admit that those propositions are believed but deny that they are true would be to state an impossibility. This would certainly seem to put metaphysics on the secure path of a science.

The first and weaker step of the Kantian strategy does not imply that. It says only that no one could consistently deny propositions whose acceptance is indispensable for thought, not that such propositions could not possibly fail to be true if believed. The difference is brought out by the well-known observation of G. E. Moore.[12] Someone who both asserts that he believes that it is raining and denies that it is raining is inconsistent in asserting what he does. The two different propositions he claims to believe are not inconsistent with each other; it is possible for someone to believe that it is raining when it is not raining. Its being believed does not imply its truth. But no one who asserts or believes both that he believes that it is raining and that it is not raining could be consistent in asserting or believing what he does.

Denying the truth of certain propositions is inconsistent with accepting those propositions. But if they are propositions whose acceptance is necessary for thought, accepting them is unavoidable for any thinker. The inconsistency that anyone who denied an indispensable proposition would fall into would show the denier to be confused or self-deceived, or to be acting somehow in bad faith, especially if he persisted in his denials.

---

12. See. E.g., G. E. Moore, "A Reply to My Critics," in P. A. Schilpp (ed.), *The Philosophy of G. E. Moore*, Tudor, New York, 1952, p. 543.

A negative metaphysical verdict about what are in fact indispensable beliefs could therefore seem to reveal the metaphysical status of their contents only if that indispensability is overlooked or forgotten or suppressed. But suppressing or avoiding or even denying that indispensability would not undermine it, and so would not eliminate the inconsistency. The indispensability confers on those beliefs a certain kind of invulnerability to metaphysical exposure or rejection. No one could consistently accept a negative metaphysical verdict about them.

The kind of invulnerability even this first step of the Kantian reasoning claims for certain elements of our conception of the world might still raise doubts about whether it could ever be established. The step involves showing, of certain specified propositions, that they must be accepted by anyone who thinks or experiences anything at all. And that looks very difficult to establish. This is the first of the two obstacles mentioned earlier.

Without denying the difficulty of establishing any such connections, I must say that I see no objection in principle. Of course one must have some conception of thought and experience, and so some idea of the minimum capacities required for thinking or experiencing anything at all. The most we can do is try to discover the conditions that must be fulfilled for even that much to be possible, and explain why thought and experience would be impossible without them. The necessary connections in question have to be argued for piecemeal, one by one, and tested against the best reasons we can find for thinking that something that looks impossible is really possible after all. But if after careful examination we find we cannot understand how anyone could think at all without thinking in certain determinate ways, or without holding certain propositions to be true, we would be in as good a position as we could be in for declaring those ways of thinking to be indispensable to any thought or experience at all.

Of course, what we state in such a judgment of necessity or indispensability is not simply that we have found it impossible to understand how someone could think without being capable of the thoughts in question. Saying that the thoughts are necessary or indispensable for any thinking at all says something more, and something stronger. But if we are right in what we say, and there is a necessary connection between thinking at all and thinking in those specified ways, that would explain our inability to make sense of the opposite; what we were trying to conceive of would really be impossible. That is just what we claim in concluding that thought is impossible without thinking in those determinate ways or holding beliefs of those specified kinds.

That judgment of a necessary connection between thinking at all and thinking in certain ways is a judgment of necessity or impossibility, and as such it might be wrong or not fully justified. It is a fallible and theo-retically revisable judgment. But all judgments, even judgments of necessity, are fallible and theoretically revisable. That does not prevent them from being true, or from being known to be true. And to know that there are certain propositions whose acceptance is necessary for any thought of a world at all would be to show that those propositions enjoy a distinctively invulnerable status in our thought about the world. No one could consistently deny them. So no one could consistently accept a negative metaphysical verdict about what those beliefs say is so.

If no negative metaphysical verdict about the contents of indispensable ways of thinking is consistently acceptable, the desire for metaphysical satisfaction can make it look as if a reassuringly positive metaphysical verdict is the only alternative. Accepting a positive verdict involves more than not accepting a negative verdict while continuing to think in those indispensable ways. That would leave the metaphysical question unresolved. The question is not simply whether we do or must think in those ways; the metaphysical status of what we thereby think about is what we want to understand. On that question, the indispensability of those ways of thinking might seem decisive, and now in favor of a reas-suringly positive verdict.

This is in effect the position of Kant. He saw the indispensability of certain ways of thinking as the only solid ground of reliable metaphys-ical knowledge of reality. But even for Kant the indispensability of those ways of thinking was not alone sufficient for a positive metaphysical verdict about their status. In the case of causation, for instance, he well understood that even Hume never doubted the *indispensability* of the concept of causation for our thought about the world.[13] Kant thought that still left open a question about what he called the 'objective validity' of the concept of causation. That is the question to which he thought Hume gave the wrong answer, or no answer at all. The full resources of the Kantian metaphysics were needed to settle that additional metaphys-ical question. It would reach beyond indispensability to the relation between the contents of those indispensable beliefs and what is so in the world.

The promise Kant saw in indispensability as the key to a satisfyingly positive answer was to be fully achieved only on the assumption of a form of idealism. I think that cannot give us the kind of positive metaphysical

---

13. Kant, *Prolegomena to Any Future Metaphysics* (tr. and ed. Gary Hatfield), Cam-bridge University Press, Cambridge, 2009, p. 8.

satisfaction we seek. But the real difficulty for this metaphysical enterprise is not simply the threat of an unacceptable idealism. I think the indispensability of certain fundamental ways of thinking presents an unavoidable obstacle to any metaphysical satisfaction of the kind we seek. That is what stands in the way of our gaining the kind of distance we need for reaching a satisfying verdict one way or the other on the metaphysical status of those ways of thinking.

For propositions whose acceptance is indispensable to any conception of a world at all, it looks as if we could never face a genuinely open question about their capturing or not capturing the way things are in the independent world. Whatever the reflections we engaged in might seem to indicate, no one could consistently accept a negative verdict about their metaphysical status. Nor could anyone consistently understand himself to have arrived at a conception of the world according to which things are not as those indispensable beliefs say they are. If we can never detach ourselves even temporarily from our acceptance of indispensable beliefs of those kinds, we could not subject them to the kind of scrutiny that an impartial metaphysical assessment of their relation to reality would seem to require. We could not be presented in metaphysical reflection with a genuinely open question on which it is even theoretically possible for us to accept one or the other of two opposed answers. Beliefs that are indispensable to any thinker's conception of a world would *have* to be retained as part of any conception that had been put under metaphysical assessment and survived. All indispensable ingredients of that original conception would *necessarily* survive any such alleged assessment.

If that is so, those indispensable beliefs would still be believed after metaphysical reflection. But they would not thereby have earned any positive metaphysical 'credit' from having 'passed' a test for capturing the way things are in reality. If indispensable beliefs could not possibly 'fail,' their 'success' or 'survival,' or their having 'passed' the metaphysical test, would show only that they are still believed. Their indispensability would simply have rendered them invulnerable to any attempt to reject them on metaphysical grounds.

It would still be possible to retain the beliefs and accept a negative metaphysical verdict about them if their contents could be shown to be equivalent to something whose truth depends in some way on the responses of human or other conscious subjects. That would show that the beliefs do not express only something that is so in a fully independent reality. This is why questions of reduction, or the sense in which one state of affairs is equivalent to, or is 'constituted by,' another play such a prominent role in metaphysical investigation.

For any reductionist strategy to succeed, some reasonable general notion of equivalence or constitution must be fixed in advance and held to. It is to no avail to appeal simply to some unexplained metaphysical conception of "what is really so" or "all that really could be so" in the world. In my own resistance to reductionism in previous chapters the only idea of non-equivalence I have relied on is the possibility of one of the allegedly equivalent statements' being true while the other is false. That is sufficient for non-equivalence, and I think it holds in each of the three cases we have considered. I do not suggest it is always an easily decidable criterion to apply, or that we are infallible in applying it. But that does not mean it cannot settle anything; and human fallibility is no reason not to do the best we can. I find in reductionism no promise of illuminating the metaphysical status of causal dependence, necessity, or values.

With beliefs that are not reducible to something whose truth depends on subjects' responses, metaphysical satisfaction seems more elusive. Accepting a negative metaphysical verdict is not consistent with continuing to accept the beliefs. To reject them on the epistemic grounds that there is no good reason to believe them, or that they have been found to be false, would be simply to change one's conception of the world, not to make a metaphysical verdict about any part of it. If the beliefs are irreducible, and are true or false independently of any actual or hypothetical responses of conscious subjects, it might seem rather that a positive metaphysical verdict about them is called for. Since their truth does not depend on human responses, it could be said that they do express the way things are in a fully independent reality.

But there is a question of what kind of illumination such an acknowledgment can provide. To say that the truth of those irreducible beliefs does not depend on conscious subjects' thinking of or responding to the world in any particular ways is to say only that propositions of those irreducible kinds do not imply any propositions of a certain other kind that we also believe. That appears to be a remark only about the relations among different ingredients of our conception of the world; propositions of one kind do not imply any propositions of a certain other kind. Metaphysics seeks more than a description of our conception of the world. To believe something, and to grant that it does not imply anything of a certain other kind, is not necessarily to take a stand on any metaphysical question.

If that were all it took, it looks as if beliefs that cannot consistently be given a negative verdict would automatically be accorded positive metaphysical status. There would then be no difference between believing something you cannot avoid believing and accepting a positive metaphysical verdict about its content. That would leave it obscure how accepting a positive metaphysical verdict about something differs from simply believing what you believe and not accepting a negative verdict about it. And then it looks as if accepting a positive metaphysical verdict would express nothing more than acceptance of an indispensable belief we regard as true. Unless a positive metaphysical verdict always wins by default, irreducible beliefs that are indispensable to thought seem as invulnerable to positive metaphysical reinforcement as they are to negative metaphysical repudiation.

For Kant the necessity or indispensability of certain ways of thinking was the key to metaphysical progress. I think that very necessity or indispensability presents an obstacle to any detached metaphysical assessment one way or the other. So what Kant saw as the first step to metaphysical satisfaction I see as an obstacle to any such satisfaction. Kant thought his step from indispensability to positive metaphysical conclusions required transcendental idealism. Without trying to reach that far, we are left at the first step only with the indispensability of certain irreducible ways of thinking. That is certainly not nothing to be left with, if there are beliefs with that distinctive status in our thought. But with idealism out of the picture, the recognition that some of our beliefs enjoy that special indispensable status yields no positive metaphysical reassurance that the world really is as those beliefs represent it to be.

Indispensability alone does not directly support metaphysical conclusions about reality because it does not amount even to the truth or known truth of the beliefs in question. The indispensability of certain beliefs renders those beliefs invulnerable to rejection: no thinker could consistently deny them. That impossibility does not imply that the beliefs in question are true, or that a positive metaphysical verdict about them is true, or that a negative metaphysical verdict is not true. The invulnerability derives from the indispensable role those beliefs play in any thinking, and so in any attempt to subject them to metaphysical assessment. It is because indispensable beliefs must be *accepted* by anyone who thinks anything that they cannot consistently be denied in the course of metaphysical reflection on their status. But that in itself does not imply that the world really is or must be as we cannot avoid believing it to be in those respects.

This is what I see as an obstacle to Kant's hopes for metaphysics. His project was to draw conclusions about the way the world is from the necessity of our having to think of the world in certain ways. I think the indispensability and metaphysical invulnerability I have been drawing attention to do not imply any metaphysical verdict about the world one way or the other. They do not take us beyond what have I called the first of the two steps of the full Kantian metaphysical project.[14] And from that alone I think no metaphysical conclusions about the nature of reality can be drawn.

In saying that the indispensability and corresponding metaphysical invulnerability of the presupposed beliefs do not imply their truth I mean only to draw attention to a failure of implication. Indispensability for thought and therefore for the metaphysical task in particular does not imply truth. That is no threat to the truth of those beliefs. It does not mean that perhaps those fundamental beliefs are not true, or that there is some reason to doubt them. The point is only that the *truth* of the beliefs we presuppose in trying to ask or pursue a metaphysical question is not what renders those beliefs invulnerable to consistent metaphysical repudiation. It is our required *acceptance* of those beliefs in acknowledging or pursuing a metaphysical question about them that accounts for their metaphysical invulnerability.

If granting the indispensability of certain beliefs for any thought of a world at all does not directly support any metaphysical verdict about the relation of those beliefs to an independent reality, we are left, at best, just where we began. All our beliefs in all their variety—about causation, necessity, values, and everything else we believe in—represent our best collective effort so far to find out what is so and why the things we believe are true. Our being unable to reach a satisfactory verdict about the metaphysical status of the things we believe in casts no aspersions on those beliefs themselves or on their credentials. We have just as much or just as little reason to accept everything we believe about the world as we had before we tried to engage in metaphysical reflection about it.

If, starting with that rich conception of the world, we find by further reflection that certain kinds of belief within it are indispensable to any thought or experience of a world at all, we can recognize the distinctive invulnerability beliefs of those kinds enjoy. But if we go on to ask in a metaphysical spirit whether beliefs of those indispensable kinds do or do not capture the ways things really are in an independent world, what kind of further satisfaction can we expect? To conclude that the beliefs must represent the way things really are because they are beliefs that any thinker must accept sounds like the familiar but hollow arrogance of idealism: things must be a certain way because we thinkers must think things are that way. But without idealism, how can we make the further step to reality?

---

14. See pp. 130–136 above.

This is not to deny that we can find that the world really is as we must believe it to be. Everything we believe expresses something we take to be true. So if we ask ourselves without preconceptions whether the world is the way the beliefs we now accept say it is, we are bound to answer 'Yes.' For every one of our beliefs we can say that things really are as that belief says things are. If there are some kinds of belief that we and all thinkers must have, we can say of those indispensable beliefs too that things are as those beliefs say things are. Since those are ways we must believe the world to be, we can say that things really are as we must believe them to be. But that is not a satisfyingly positive answer to a metaphysical question about the relation between our indispensable beliefs and an independent reality. It is a mundane observation we are always in a position to make, without any metaphysical reflection. As far as we have been able to tell so far, the world is just the way we now believe it (or even must believe it) to be.

To say that we think the world really is as we now believe it to be does not mean that we regard our current conception of the world as fixed or untouchable. It does not mean that we cannot subject that conception to critical assessment and reject those parts of it that we think do not capture the way things really are. That is a task we are engaged in all the time. We reject some things as false or unjustified and so eliminate them from our conception of the world, or never admit them into it in the first place. That is part of the continuous epistemic enterprise of adjusting our beliefs to the way things are. I do not mean to suggest that it is easy, or uncomplicated. But metaphysical assessment of our conception of the world comes later, when some such conception has already been accepted, even if tentatively. Only then is there a subject matter for a distinctively metaphysical investigation to focus on. It is that critical second-level metaphysical enterprise that I think faces the obstacles I have been trying to identify.

6

Metaphysical Dissatisfaction

I have been drawing attention to the dissatisfaction that metaphysical reflection of the kind we have been concerned with appears to leave us with. I think its source lies in our unavoidable immersion in whatever conception of the world we seek metaphysical understanding of. That is what prevents us from finding enough distance between our conception of the world and the world it is meant to be a conception of to allow for an appropriately impartial metaphysical verdict on the relation between the two. Metaphysics must proceed 'from within.' We must start from the conception of the world we already have, as expressed in everything we now believe to be so. But then it appears to be too late to achieve the kind of metaphysical understanding we seek.

Starting from within does not mean we cannot come to reject some of the beliefs we hold. We can do so by questioning their epistemic credentials and qualifying certain beliefs or eliminating them from our conception of the world. That is part of our continuous epistemic effort to adjust the things we believe to what we take to be the best available reasons for believing them. That would be to revise our conception, not to reach a negative metaphysical verdict about some part of it. Any metaphysical reflection we engaged in would then be directed toward that new conception.

We have seen how the indispensability of certain beliefs for any thought of a world at all would bring the significance of what looks like a metaphysical verdict about those beliefs into question. I have tried to bring out in each case how our causal beliefs, our beliefs in necessity, and our evaluative beliefs are all invulnerable to consistent metaphysical repudiation. But beliefs can be invulnerable to a negative metaphysical verdict even if they are not absolutely indispensable to all thought of a world at all. Invulnerability derives from indispensability, and beliefs can be indispensable for metaphysical reflection, and so invulnerable to consistent metaphysical repudiation, in different ways or for different reasons.

Beliefs that have to be accepted by anyone who is faced with a metaphysical question about their status would be metaphysically invulnerable. This can happen in considering one's own beliefs. Raising a question about the relation between our beliefs about the world and the world those beliefs are about can leave us without the reflective distance to answer the question with anything other than a flatfooted 'Yes'; the two will correspond completely. But the same obstacle can arise in considering the beliefs of others. To reflect on others' beliefs, we must at least acknowledge the beliefs that other people hold. There has to be *some* conception of the world whose metaphysical credentials we want to investigate. So any conception of the world we start with and try to reach metaphysical conclusions about will include human beings and their experiences and thoughts and beliefs and actions.

This means that in metaphysical reflection on any conception of the world we must fulfill the conditions of acknowledging the presence of the thoughts and beliefs and experiences that make up that conception. One condition of doing that is that we understand the contents of the thoughts and beliefs we acknowledge. We must recognize what the thoughts and beliefs in question actually are. And that requires that we possess the concepts used to express the beliefs we acknowledge, whether we accept those beliefs or not. Understanding that there is a world of thinkers and believers responding to the world in ways we can make sense of requires a rich and complex set of capacities. It is not something obvious and easily open to view. It is here that I think we begin to approach the real source of the inevitable metaphysical dissatisfaction.

One question that bears directly on the prospects of the metaphysical enterprise is whether there are certain things we must *believe* about the world even to understand and acknowledge the psychological facts of thought and belief we would subject to metaphysical assessment. If so, those presupposed beliefs will be indispensable to that metaphysical reflection; if we did not accept them we could not even acknowledge the beliefs we want to investigate. But then those beliefs will be invulnerable to consistent metaphysical repudiation by anyone who seeks a verdict about their metaphysical status.

There is reason to think some beliefs will always be presupposed in this way in any metaphysical reflection. To understand beliefs of a certain kind we must possess the concepts needed to express the contents of those beliefs. If concepts are "predicates of possible judgements," as Kant held, then to possess and understand a certain concept is to have a capacity to make certain kinds of judgments in which that concept is deployed. We must be able to judge or put forward as true thoughts in which the concepts we possess play an essential role.

The capacity for judgment involved in possessing or understanding a concept has sometimes been thought to be a capacity only for a priori judgment of those 'analytic' or necessary truths that hold solely in virtue of what is "contained" in the "content" of the concept. Possession of the concept of a bachelor, for instance, involves knowing a priori that necessarily all bachelors are unmarried men. But it is implausible to say that is all that is involved in understanding or possessing a concept, even without questioning the doctrine of analyticity. Granting that the statements of arithmetic, for instance, are 'analytic,' there is still a question whether someone can be said to fully understand the concept of natural number, or the number four in particular, if he could never recognize, for example, that there are four apples on the table, or that if another apple were added, there would be five. Knowing such things is knowledge of how things contingently are or would be in the world, not just knowledge of 'analytic' truths of arithmetic. Someone who knew no such contingent facts, or lacked the capacity to come to know such things in the appropriate circumstances, could not be said to fully understand or possess the concept of number.

The same holds for a great many other concepts; knowing or believing that things stand in a certain way in the world is essential to possessing or understanding them, even if things' being that way is not implied by the contents of the concept itself. With the concept of causation, for instance, it is not enough to understand only the abstract formal properties of causal judgments and how they differ in their modality and their implications from statements of mere coincidence. One must be able to judge on appropriate occasions that this caused that or that if such-and-such kind of thing were to happen so-and-so would be the result. Someone who was incapable of making such applications of the concept we use in our causal judgments would not be a proficient causal thinker. He would be unable to come to believe or understand that one thing happened because another thing happened. But such judgments, if they are true, are not 'analytic' judgments simply expressing the 'content' of the concept of causation.

One's possession and grasp of the concept of 'absolute' necessity is also exhibited in one's applications of it, in judging, for example, that if *this* is true then *that* must be true. Whether that holds or not in a particular case depends on what is said or implied by the thoughts in question; it is not discovered simply by reflection on the very 'content' of the idea of necessity.

With the concept of value, or of such-and-such being reason to believe or do so-and-so, the point is perhaps clearest. It is difficult to say what the possession of that concept of a reason amounts to *except* the capacity to take certain things as reason to believe or act in certain ways. There seems to be no question of stating the 'content' of that concept in some different but equivalent terms. The capacity to apply the concept is involved in the possession and understanding of *all* concepts. Applying or withholding the concept 'four' or 'cause' or 'reason' or any other concept in appropriate circumstances requires recognizing in those circumstances something that is reason to apply or withhold the concept in question. That is not simply a matter of making an 'analytic' judgment of a necessary truth expressing part of the 'content' of the concept 'reason for . . . '

If possession and understanding concepts requires a capacity to judge, in the appropriate circumstances, that the concept applies, or does not apply, to something, anyone who has such a capacity will therefore have, or be capable of getting, some beliefs of that kind if the appropriate circumstances present themselves. It is not that there are some specific beliefs about the world that anyone who has the concept of causation or necessity or value must hold. Competence with those concepts implies only that one accepts some beliefs or other in which the concepts are correctly applied to what is so in the world. Continually failing to respond appropriately in one's own voice in the right circumstances would count against one's possessing or fully understanding the concept in question.

This means that anyone who understands and attributes beliefs of a certain kind to others must have, or be capable of getting, some beliefs of the kinds she shares with other believers she understands. We need not agree with all or perhaps any of the specific beliefs we take other believers to accept. For instance, we might think that many causal beliefs held by other believers are not in fact correct. But for us to have that thought we must understand those others to have causal beliefs, and so to have the concept of causal dependence. In that respect, we will share a general conception of a causally ordered world with those others, however much we disagree about the details. If having the concept involves holding some causal beliefs, and that in turn is indispensable to our recognizing even false beliefs of that kind in others, we could not consistently arrive at a negative metaphysical verdict about causal dependence in general by reflecting on those others' causal beliefs. This will be so even if causal beliefs are not indispensable to any thought of a world at all. The same holds for our beliefs in necessity and our evaluative beliefs. Wide divergences among us about which truths hold necessarily or what is reason to believe or do what are compatible with everyone's agreeing that some things hold necessarily and some things are reason to do or believe something.

This background of agreement represents no obstacle to metaphysical satisfaction if the beliefs we presuppose or share with others are not beliefs of the kind to which we direct our metaphysical attention. If the status of causal dependence or necessity or evaluation is not what is in question, for instance, our sharing causal or necessary or evaluative beliefs with other believers we can understand would be no obstacle to arriving at negative metaphysical verdicts about beliefs of other kinds. But when the beliefs we must hold even to recognize what is to be subjected to metaphysical assessment are beliefs of the very kind that we seek a metaphysical verdict about, we cannot then get the satisfaction we are after. We cannot consistently accept a negative metaphysical verdict to the effect that the independent world is *not* in general as beliefs of that kind say it is. That would be ruled out by our fulfilling the conditions for possessing the concepts needed even to face the problem. And simply continuing to accept beliefs of that kind, even with very good reasons to accept them, would give no support to a satisfyingly positive metaphysical verdict either. We would not have reached a satisfying verdict one way or the other. And this can be true even of beliefs that are not absolutely indispensable to any thought of a world at all.

I have argued that this is true of our beliefs about the colors of things.[1] I do not think beliefs about the colors of things, for all their interest and importance for us, are indispensable to any thought of a world at all. We could inhabit and make sense of an independent world even if we were blind and could see nothing, and so had no concepts of the colors of things. But to recognize that people do see colors and have corresponding beliefs about the colors of objects, and so to be faced with a metaphysical question about the status of those beliefs, we must understand thoughts about the colors of things.

Possessing concepts of the colors of things requires a capacity to judge in appropriate circumstances that objects around us have such-and-such colors. So with normal human capacities, and the opportunities the world normally presents us with, we will inevitably have or get beliefs about the colors of the things we see around us. We need not

---

1. See my *The Quest for Reality: Subjectivism and the Metaphysics of Colour*, Oxford University Press, New York, 2000, esp. chs. 6, 7.

share each particular color belief or even any of a large class of color beliefs with those we understand to have such beliefs of their own, but we will share beliefs to the effect that objects are some color or other, and so the very general belief that objects are colored. Faced with a question we can understand about the colors of things in general, we could not consistently accept the negative metaphysical verdict that no objects are colored in independent reality.

A negative verdict might seem reachable by showing that all beliefs about the colors of objects are reducible to statements only about dispositions objects have to produce distinctive perceptions of color in perceivers of various kinds under certain conditions. That would show that the truth of beliefs about the colors of things depends on certain things' being true of human perceivers. But if acknowledging and making sense of people even as having *perceptions* of particular colors requires possession of concepts of the colors of objects, and that in turn requires a capacity to judge in the appropriate circumstances that objects are this or that color, the reality of the colors of things could not be consistently 'unmasked' in that way. The putative reduction would be intelligible to us only if we have some beliefs about the colors of things.

The unacceptability of a negative verdict for that reason does not imply a positive metaphysical verdict about the reality of the colors of things. We would simply be left with our metaphysically invulnerable belief that objects are colored. I think this is also the position we are left in with our beliefs in causal dependence, necessity, and values. If beliefs of those kinds are not reducible to any alternative set of concepts that do not presuppose them, as I think they are not, we cannot reach a negative verdict about them by reducing them to something whose truth depends on subjects' responses. Nor can we consistently accept a negative verdict about them if possessing those irreducible concepts, and so holding some beliefs involving them, is required even to raise a metaphysical question about them. They will be invulnerable in that way to consistent metaphysical repudiation even if they are not absolutely indispensable to all thought.

Beliefs can also be invulnerable to consistent metaphysical repudiation by being presupposed, not in the very acknowledgment of a metaphysical question about them, but in the attempt to answer that question in a certain way. Descartes's 'Cogito' is absolutely invulnerable to repudiation in the strongest sense. It cannot be truly denied by the thinker. Because denying something is itself a form of thinking, any attempt to deny it is sufficient for the truth of what is denied. I cannot truly deny in any way that I am thinking.

I cannot, by speaking, truly deny that I am speaking either: that way of trying to deny it guarantees its truth, as with 'Cogito.' But there are other ways I can truly deny that I am speaking; by writing or holding up a sign, for instance. So it is not absolutely impossible for me to truly deny that I am speaking. Whether I can succeed or not depends on how I try to do it. In the case of 'Cogito' there is no way at all to do it. With 'I am speaking' I can do it in several ways, but there is one way in which it is impossible. Comparable obstacles can arise in metaphysical reflection.

When what is in question is not the truth of a belief, as with 'Cogito,' but only whether the belief could be consistently rejected, as with the metaphysical verdicts we have been considering, beliefs can enjoy this kind of relative metaphysical invulnerability. That will be so when acceptance of the beliefs is required in the particular kind of metaphysical reasoning by which a verdict about them is to be reached. We saw an instance of this in the effort to reach a negative metaphysical verdict about causal dependence by offering an explanation of how we come to believe in it even though there really are no such connections between things in the independent world.[2] If an explanation of something by appeal to something else requires not just a (possibly accidental) correlation between the two, but some modally expressed connection between them, that attempt to explain our causal beliefs makes essential use of the very idea of causal dependence it was meant to repudiate. No negative metaphysical verdict about causal dependence in general could consistently be reached by that 'unmasking' strategy.

This shows only that a negative metaphysical verdict about causal dependence is not consistently acceptable if arrived at by that route. It does not follow that a negative verdict about causation cannot be consistently reached in any way at all. That would be so if the belief is essential to any thought of a world at all. But even if that is not so, and acceptance of the belief is indispensable only to a particular way of arriving at a verdict about its metaphysical status, the belief is invulnerable to consistent rejection by that attempt. In fact, if belief in causal dependence is essential to *any* attempt to explain how we come to believe in it, it could never be consistently 'unmasked' as unreal by any such explanation.

Accepting some beliefs of each of the three kinds we have been focusing on is essential to metaphysical reflection on their status and their relation to reality. Their necessary involvement either in our facing a metaphysical question or in conducting reflections directed toward reaching a metaphysical verdict about them prevents us from successfully completing the reflective task; we cannot consistently arrive at a negative metaphysical verdict about beliefs that are presupposed in those ways.

---

2. See pp. 32–34 above.

I think there is a deeper or more general reason for the metaphysical invulnerability of beliefs of the fundamental kinds we have been considering. Accepting some beliefs of each kind is indispensable even for acknowledging the presence in the world of any thoughts or beliefs at all, whatever they might be about. If we did not believe in causal dependence, in necessity, and in something's being reason to believe or do something, we could not understand and believe in the kinds of psychological facts we take to be part of the world, and from which our metaphysical reflections begin.

When reflecting metaphysically on the scope and limits of reality as it is independently of us and our responses to it, it is perhaps easy to overlook the significance of including thinkers with perceptions, thoughts, and beliefs within one's conception of what is so in the world. Metaphysical reflection tends to concentrate on how such things as causal dependence, necessity, or value are to be accommodated within, or otherwise somehow excluded from, what we already take to be so in the independent world. This involves our thinking of ourselves as *thinking* of the world in those 'richer' ways we are interested in, while asking or wondering whether the world really contains any such metaphysically 'richer' states of affairs.

Since it can then seem possible for us to believe what we do about causal dependence, necessity, and values without there being any facts of those kinds in the independent world, that possibility encourages the hope of arriving at a negative verdict about the real metaphysical status of those apparently 'richer' beliefs. Either their contents are to be reduced to something that is part of the more austere world we already accept, or our believing them is to be explained away without committing ourselves to anything corresponding to them in the independent world.

But it is not enough that we, equipped as we now are with those 'richer' ways of thinking, can form, or think we can form, a conception of the world in which we hold those 'richer' beliefs even though they represent nothing that is really so in that world. It must be shown that a more austere world that lacks those 'richer' ingredients nonetheless contains within it the materials needed to account for our having the beliefs we actually have.[3] That human beings think and believe the kinds of things we do must be intelligible as part of the world we actually live in.

---

3. Here I explicitly invoke P. F. Strawson's way of describing the strategy he follows to such illuminating metaphysical effect with the apparent possibility of a purely 'sense-datum' conception of experience (*The Bounds of Sense*, Methuen, London, 1966, p. 109). My own way of treating the kind of metaphysical project I consider here is greatly indebted to Strawson throughout.

A conception of an independent world so austere as not to mention human perceivers or believers or agents at all would not be an adequate conception of the world we live in. It is not a conception of the world that anyone could even have if the world were only as that conception says it is. It leaves no room for anyone's having the thoughts and beliefs we actually have as things are—the very thoughts and beliefs we need to engage in metaphysical reflection on their status.

But if we acknowledge human agents with thoughts and beliefs within our conception of the world, we must fulfill all the necessary conditions of thinking of the world in those psychological ways. If that requires that we also think of the world in certain other ways as well, our conception of the world will have to include whatever else we have to believe to be so in acknowledging those psychological facts of thought and belief. This raises the question of what else has to be added. What additional kinds of beliefs must we hold if our conception of the world is to contain human beings who perceive and think about the world in determinate ways?

This is not directly a question about what the world we thereby think about must be like. It is not a question about what must be so in any world that contains psychological facts of thought and belief. The question is rather what else we must *believe* the world to be like if we acknowledge determinate thoughts and beliefs as part of that world. If we are to reflect metaphysically on the status of some of the things we believe in, there must be thinkers with thoughts and beliefs in the world we live in. That is something we could not consistently deny. To say that we therefore must believe certain other things about the world in order to acknowledge those psychological facts is not to say that those other things we must believe must be *true*. But we must *believe* them to be true if their acceptance is required in acknowledging (what we cannot consistently deny) that there are psychological facts of thought and belief in the world.

From the fact that we must accept those additional beliefs we cannot conclude that they are therefore true. So no positive conclusions about the world would be forthcoming from our fulfilling this requirement. Not because the beliefs in question are not or would not be true, but because their truth does not follow from the fact that we must believe them. But it does follow, for reasons we have seen, that we could not consistently accept a general negative metaphysical verdict about the contents of those presupposed beliefs. We could not consistently accept a verdict that denies or repudiates something the acceptance of which is required for acknowledging thoughts and beliefs as part of the world. That is because no one engaged in metaphysical reflection could consistently deny the presence in the world of some such psychological facts.

The impossibility of truly denying 'Cogito' confers that same impossibility of true denial on anything else that must be true if 'Cogito' is true. The impossibility of consistently denying that there is thinking or believing in the world confers that same impossibility of consistent denial on anything else that must be accepted in accepting that there are such psychological facts of thought or belief. Everything we must believe in believing that there are such psychological facts in the world would be invulnerable in that way to consistent metaphysical repudiation. Reflection on the conditions of acknowledging a world of thinkers and believers responding to the world in ways we make sense of would reveal the metaphysical invulnerability of whatever beliefs are indispensable for the acknowledgement of those psychological facts.

I think beliefs in causal dependence, in necessity, and in something's being reason to believe or to do something are in general metaphysically invulnerable for this reason. Some beliefs of each of the three fundamental kinds are among the beliefs I think we must accept if we think of the world as containing thinkers with perceptions of and beliefs about the world. Any attempt at detached or non-committal reflection on the relation between our beliefs and the world they are about is possible only because we are committed to the truth of some beliefs of the very kinds we attempt to bring under metaphysical scrutiny. That would explain the metaphysical invulnerability of beliefs of those kinds.

We understand people as believing the sorts of things they do in large part because of the way the world they perceive and think about affects them. That is a causal connection. We make sense of people as having the thoughts and beliefs we take them to have by understanding how their thinking and believing what they do is connected with the way the world is. We also believe that the world we take to have such effects on believers is in large part independent of its being believed to be any particular way; it would have been more or less the way it is even if no one had ever believed anything. That is causal independence, or the negation of causal dependence, between beliefs and the non-psychological world. The actions of believing agents have widespread effects on what the world is like, but believings alone have no such direct or pervasive influence.

The non-psychological world we believe to stand in these relations to psychological phenomena like perceptions and beliefs is understood to have a causal, law-like structure and to contain relatively enduring physical objects with stable properties and dispositions that make their behavior intelligible. That is how it can have the effects on perceivers and thinkers we believe it to have, and how it can also remain independent of its being thought about by those thinkers in those ways. Our acceptance of beliefs in causal dependence and independence is inextricably involved in acknowledging thinkers, believers, and agents as part of the world.

The idea of 'absolute' necessity is at least equally deeply embedded in our acknowledging the presence of minds. There is no necessity between the world being a certain way and its being believed to be that way; it is possible for the world to have been more or less as it is without anyone's having any beliefs at all. And from the fact that someone, or even everyone, believes something, it does not in general follow that it is true. We recognize thought and the world to stand in these relations to each other only because we have the ideas of necessity and possibility. That is what enables us to recognize the possibility of false belief, and so to understand knowledge or reasonable true belief as an achievement, something beyond mere belief.

Our very understanding of thought itself also involves the idea of necessity. Anyone who thinks something must be capable of moving from one thought to another, and so capable of recognizing relations among distinct thoughts. A thinker must sometimes know or believe that a certain thought he entertains could, or must, be true if a certain other thought is true. We could make no sense of someone who thinks but never recognizes any such possibilities or necessities. We make use of the idea of necessity, and so hold certain things to be necessarily true, both in thinking of others as believers and in our believing things ourselves about the non-psychological world.

Evaluative beliefs are perhaps most deeply involved in our acknowledging thinkers, believers, and agents as part of the world. Believing something or acting intentionally involves taking something as a reason to believe, accept, or deny something, or to intend, prefer, or endorse something. We could not understand thinkers or agents as believing or doing things for reasons if we did not understand them as taking certain things they are aware of to be reasons to believe or do what they do. Not only must they have evaluative attitudes; we must ascribe such attitudes to them to understand them as believers or agents. And we as ascribers of such attitudes, and so as believers, must have some such attitudes ourselves.

Accepting evaluative judgments to the effect that such-and-such is reason to believe or to do a certain thing is indispensable not only in making sense of others as thinkers and agents, but in any thinking by which anyone comes to believe or do something for reasons. All thinking directed toward finding out what is so or what to do requires considering and responding to whatever reasons can be found for believing or doing the things in question. It requires evaluative judgment. Since this holds for any attempt to reach a conclusion about anything, it holds in particular for acknowledging that there are thinkers and agents in the world.[4] But it also holds for any thinking involved in metaphysical reflection. I think this is the real source of the impossibility of anyone's consistently accepting a negative metaphysical verdict about evaluative judgments in general.

The conclusion I think we are left with is that metaphysical reflection on beliefs of the three kinds we have considered is possible only if we also accept some beliefs of the kinds we wish to bring into question. That does not necessarily carry with it the truth of any of those beliefs, but it does carry with it acceptance of everything that must be accepted in acknowledging that we have beliefs of those kinds. When we go on to ask about the truth or the relation to reality of any of those additional beliefs we could not consistently accept a negative answer about them while continuing to accept the psychological fact that we believe them. And to go so far as to deny the contents of all beliefs of those kinds would be to fall into the inconsistency I think a negative metaphysical verdict about beliefs of those fundamental kinds inevitably leaves us in. We would hold that we believe certain things while denying the very things we say we believe.

This would be metaphysically disappointing. It would not fulfill our metaphysical hopes. In his *Prolegomena* Kant asked why, if metaphysics is not or cannot ever be a systematic body of reliable knowledge of the world, it continually presents itself as being such a 'science,' and "strings along the human understanding with hopes that never fade but are never fulfilled?"[5] Kant thought hopes had never been fulfilled because there had never been a 'critique of pure reason' that explains how metaphysics is possible and puts it once and for all on the sure path of a science. That is what he tried to do.

But what explains the fact that our hopes "never fade" even if we find they have not been fulfilled? Why does metaphysics as a reliable, systematic body of knowledge continue to seem not only possible but available? What I have been suggesting perhaps points in the direction of an answer that is at least partly Kantian. Metaphysics can seem to offer the prospect of reliable knowledge because we raise what we take to be

---

4. This is the source of the obstacles Gibbard recognizes in attempting to 'elucidate' evaluative thinking in general in exclusively non-evaluative 'naturalistic' terms. See pp. 120–124 above.

5. Kant, *Prolegomena to Any Future Metaphysics* (trans. and ed. Gary Hatfield), Cambridge University Press, Cambridge, 2009, p. 5.

straightforward questions about the relation between some of our fundamental beliefs and reality while neglecting the necessary conditions of
our possessing the relevant concepts and so holding some of the very
beliefs that present us with those questions in the first place. We thereby
misconstrue the nature, and therefore the prospects, of the inquiry we
undertake. It is not only in metaphysics that this tendency can be found
in philosophy, and with similar results.

We make sense of ourselves as fully engaged in thinking and acting in
a world in which some things are causally dependent on others, some
things hold necessarily, some things are good reason to believe or do certain things, and human beings believe many things of all those kinds to
be so. The metaphysical project starts from this broadly speaking psychological part of our conception of the world—our believing the kinds of
things we do—and asks how the things we thereby believe are related to
the rest of what is really so. But we have seen that there is a question
whether we can successfully separate that portion of our conception of
the world in that way from all the rest of what we believe. We obviously
can attend to that purely psychological portion alone for this or that particular purpose. But can we separate it from all the rest with the prospect
of arriving at a satisfyingly open-minded assessment of the metaphysical
status of those things we believe? This is what I think we cannot do.

Taking up metaphysical questions about reality without reflecting on
the conditions of our asking them or making sense of them can make it
look as if they are questions to be answered, as it seems all legitimate
questions are to be answered, simply by careful investigation of the relevant domain by the most appropriate means. We have beliefs about the
constitution of matter, for instance, or about distant planets, or about
events in the ancient world, and we look to the relevant parts of reality
to find out what is so or whether what we believe about them is something we should continue to believe. We ask and seek answers to those
questions without thinking it appropriate to inquire into the necessary
conditions of our possessing the relevant concepts and understanding
and holding the beliefs in question.

We also can see on reflection that we believe that some things are causally dependent on others, that some things hold necessarily, and that some
things are reason to believe or to do certain things, and those beliefs, while
admittedly more general than the others, can also seem to invite the same
kind of straightforward investigation. We ask about the relation between
what we thereby believe and the way things are in reality without considering the necessary conditions of our having or understanding any such
beliefs. In this way, metaphysics can present itself as just one among many
more or less general kinds of investigation of what is really so.

But that appearance will be a misleading and will simply "string along the human understanding" if the kinds of beliefs that are of metaphysical interest are fundamental to thinking of any world at all, or are essential to thinking of a world as containing beings who think about the world. If the acceptance of some beliefs of the three kinds we have been concerned with is presupposed even in acknowledging that we think about the world at all, no one's hopes for metaphysical satisfaction about those beliefs could be fulfilled by a negative verdict about their relation to independent reality. But if Kant is right that even unfulfilled hopes for metaphysics "never fade," it looks as if those hopes could be satisfied, if at all, only by accepting a positive metaphysical verdict.

I have tried to show that no such positive metaphysical verdict about the status in independent reality of causal dependence, necessity, and something's being a reason to believe or do something follows from the impossibility of consistently accepting a negative verdict about them. Nor does any such verdict follow from anything else we have discovered about those beliefs. And aside from the question of what supports it, there is also the question of what any such a verdict says, and what is involved in accepting it. A positive metaphysical verdict must differ in some way from everything we believe that is expressed in causal, modal, and evaluative terms. It seems possible to hold beliefs of those kinds with no metaphysical opinions one way or the other. What then would a positive metaphysical verdict add to what is already expressed in those beliefs? How would it contribute to our understanding of the world?

A positive metaphysical verdict could at least seem to offer what a negative verdict promised but could not deliver: a detached, impartial, and consistently acceptable account of the relation between the beliefs in question and the independent reality they are about. To say that independent reality *is* as we believe it to be in those fundamental respects could even seem reassuring. But how satisfying or reassuring would that verdict really be?

For one thing, if modal and evaluative notions are felt to be metaphysically problematic when the metaphysical question about them is first raised, and those fundamental concepts are irreducible to any notions that do not presuppose them, as I believe they are, then even a positive verdict would seem to offer no prospect of increasing our metaphysical understanding. There would be no possibility of discovering by further reflection what there is in reality "in virtue of which" those modal and evaluative beliefs are true. Illumination would be possible on that point if the contents of the beliefs could be reduced to states of affairs that do not hold in independent reality alone, but that would yield a negative metaphysical verdict, and would deny the irreducibility of the beliefs in question. Accepting a positive verdict, along with the irreducibility of the beliefs, would seem to leave us with modal and evaluative facts as simply otherwise inexplicable aspects of reality. And if that is how they seemed at the beginning, we would remain dissatisfied, having made no metaphysical advance.

It looks as if we would be in just as good a position for understanding what is so in the world by accepting whatever irreducibly modal and evaluative beliefs we find to be well-supported while asking no further metaphysical questions about them. In each of the cases we have considered we have found it difficult to say in so many words what we would then be missing. Being unable to say unambiguously what the metaphysical question asks, or what a positive metaphysical verdict says, can encourage the thought that there is no meaningful metaphysical 'question' or 'answer.' This was the view of the logical positivists, on the strength of a conception of meaning eventually to be defined in terms of a by-now largely discredited theory of knowledge. But you do not have to be a logical positivist to feel that when everything has been said causally and modally and evaluatively about the way things are, there is nothing metaphysical left to be said. Whatever questions remain are to be answered by further causal or modal or evaluative inquiry.

This robust response, for all its appeal, is not where I think we can stop in the attempt to understand metaphysical reflections of the kind we have been concerned with. There is a metaphysical urge, or need, that cannot be denied, however difficult it is to express it in unambiguous terms. It is present, I believe, in our recognizing even so much as a general question about the status of judgments of beauty, for instance, or evaluative judgments, and in our feeling the pull of a negative metaphysical verdict in those cases. I think most of us can feel that pull, and so can be inclined in the direction of a negative answer even if we admit we have on hand no remotely plausible reductive account of the contents of the judgments in question. There is a feeling that a negative verdict is so obviously called for that there simply must be a satisfactory reductive account or explanation, even if no one has found it yet.

Many are equally tempted by metaphysical verdicts one way or the other about causal dependence and 'absolute' necessity. They thereby show that they acknowledge a metaphysical question in those cases too. What is of interest at this point is not how or whether such verdicts are to be shown to be right, or wrong. What is remarkable is the strength of the widespread feeling that things simply must be metaphysically one way or the other. That conviction, above all, is what I think reveals the presence of a certain metaphysical urge or aspiration. It shows that, for those parts of our conception of the world concerned with causal dependence, necessity, and evaluative matters, something more is thought to be required for a full understanding the world and our relation to it than amply warranted acceptance or even knowledge of the truth of beliefs of those kinds.

Those metaphysical questions and aspirations are material for philosophy if anything is. Acknowledging and confronting them is central to the way philosophy can contribute to an understanding of ourselves and the world. It is widely felt that not to answer the metaphysical questions one way or the other, or even to try to answer them, however tentatively, would be simple evasion, an avoidance of philosophy, even a kind of betrayal of its calling. Not taking a metaphysical stand one way or the other looks to many philosophers like nothing more than anti-theoretical indifference—a refusal to take on what is in fact a serious intellectual challenge to any deeply thinking person.

But accepting or even leaning toward a positive or a negative answer to a metaphysical question is not the only way to contribute to philosophical understanding of ourselves. There is at least one other possibility. Someone who is inclined to neither metaphysical answer is not necessarily avoiding serious philosophical reflection or denying the significance of the metaphysical aspiration. One possible outcome of philosophical reflection could be the realization that in the search for a completely general understanding of ourselves in relation to the independent world *no* metaphysical satisfaction is possible one way or the other. That too is a possible result of careful examination of the thoughts we wish to subject to metaphysical assessment. It is a state we might achieve while acknowledging and understanding the source of the obstacles that preclude the kind of metaphysical understanding of those beliefs that we seek. That is the possibility I have tried to illustrate and to recommend for further exploration.

If it could be shown that no metaphysical satisfaction is possible in the way we seek it, and we could understand why that is so, that itself could be a significant fact about the human condition. It would not give us what metaphysical reflection seemed to promise, but it might provide a certain reflective or second-level satisfaction of its own. We would recognize that we seek a certain kind of detached understanding of ourselves and the world that we also can see we can never achieve. If some such conclusion is to be reached, and appreciated, it will not be by avoiding philosophical reflection. An understanding of ourselves even without a metaphysical verdict one way or the other cannot be reached and found convincing without the careful, thorough intellectual effort that is called for in any serious philosophical investigation.

Index